Praise for *Results Rule!*

"What on earth could pre-thawed turkeys, Eva the dolphin, and toothpaste tubes squeezed from the middle have to do with the success of your business? Everything. *Results Rule!* is that rare business book that you can't put down, and you shouldn't, because the lessons within aren't just helpful, they're vitally important. Don't put *Results Rule!* on the stack of books you mean to read soon. Buy it, take it home, and read every word before your competitor does."

> Joe Calloway
> Author, *Indispensable: How to Become the Company That Your Customers Can't Live Without*

"Most business books give you everything you need and want to do, except the only thing that matters—getting results. This book is well-written, with great examples, stories and real advice, that will actually show you how to improve your results. Buy it—read it—heed it—and watch your results improve."

> Larry Winget
> Author, *Shut Up, Stop Whining & Get a Life!*

"*Results Rule!* delivers practical ideas that will keep your organization on course for success in a competitive marketplace. Randy Pennington offers ideas that work if you are on the front-line or in the executive suite. He has nailed the essence and importance of culture."

> Howard Putnam
> Former CEO, Southwest Airlines
> Author, *The Winds of Turbulence*

"If you hate your competition, it's because they're beating you. If you want your competition to hate YOU—read Randy Pennington's book, and give it to all your people."

> Jeffrey Gitomer
> Author, *The Little Red Book of Selling*

"Six rock solid concepts + real examples in a quick and easy read = real results. A guide to differentiating your organization in the market place."

"Randy's business savvy and expertise are evident throughout this book. His thoughtful analyses produce vital points for any business that wants to grow and thrive in the 21st century."

"In a very engaging, quick read, Randy Pennington cuts through the hype of most management bestsellers to propose a deceptively simple premise—a culture that never loses focus on the desired result and always wins. Pennington takes you by the hand and shows you how to take an honest look at your own organization, then act immediately to create and nurture a culture that achieves results day in and day out. *Results Rule!* is one of those rare books you'll keep close at hand for years to come."

"If you believe 'Results Rule,' then you'll find that this book rocks. Randy Pennington has boiled down his years of experiences and insights into a book that is packed with concrete examples and more importantly, shows you how you and your organization can rule by creating superior results. If you want more and better results, then read this book."

"*Results Rule!* is an incredible formula for success. Randy Pennington raises questions, delivers answers, and challenges you to a higher level of leadership. Execute these ideas and your organization will rule!"

> Lisa Ford
> Author, *How to Give Exceptional Customer Service*

"This much common sense is definitely uncommon. Any company or organization that wants to succeed and achieve a *Results Rule!* mentality should read and apply the lessons from this book."

> Gary Nelon
> Chairman and CEO
> First Texas Bancorp, Inc.

"Pennington reveals how to create a results culture in your organization. Powerful, provocative, must-read material for all serious leaders."

> Randy Gage
> Author, *Prosperity Mind*

"Randy Pennington, once again, hits straight at the heart of the issue. He avoids the myth that performance management and building a great culture has to be *easy* and *simple*; it isn't. It is complex. But it can *become* a competitive advantage for those who are willing to accept accountability and invest the time to practice the truly important skills; for them, the results will come—deservedly so."

> Clinton Wingrove
> Managing Director, Pilat NAI

"Randy Pennington has captured the essence of business culture required to succeed in today's global market. Make sure your highlighter is within reach for the entire book as Mr. Pennington's advice on successful business culture emanates from Preface to Post Notes. If your business is in need of an injection of new life, transform your company culture with this sound, accountability-driven advice."

> Tom Haag
> President and COO, SGS Tool

"There is something here for everyone. The ability to influence others and/or one's organizational culture is not limited to the senior management. Everyone has that ability. And organizational culture is at the heart of an organization's ability to be successful. I really enjoyed this book, I hope you will too."

Eric Schlesinger
Author, *e-Job Hunting*

"Articulating, nurturing and protecting an authentic culture that inspires and gives guidance is the difference between having a good year and building a great, enduring company. *Results Rule!* shows how the right corporate culture makes all the difference in a marketplace where products and services are increasingly seen as interchangeable. It is filled with powerful yet simple truths, insights, and practical advice to help leaders and the organizations they serve succeed year after year after year."

Henry S. Givray
Chairman and CEO, SmithBucklin Corporation

"One of the most useful and engaging business books I've read in some time. Well worth your time and money. Keep your pen handy, you'll be underlining a lot!"

Ian Percy
Author, *Going Deep: Exploring Spirituality in Life & Leadership*

"Through stories and examples taken from a career in business and consulting, Randy Pennington presents a practical framework for professional and organizational success through a focus on culture and results. I walked away with a half-dozen hard hitting action items in one afternoon reading. Wish I had had this book 13 years ago when founding Bridgeway."

John Montgomery
Founder, Bridgeway Mutual Funds

RESULTS RULE!

RESULTS RULE!

Build a Culture That Blows the Competition Away

RANDY PENNINGTON

WILEY

JOHN WILEY & SONS, INC.

Published by John Wiley & Sons, Inc., Hoboken, New Jersey.
Published simultaneously in Canada.

For general information on our other products and services or for technical support, please contact our Customer Care Department within the United States at (800) 762-2974, outside the United States at (317) 572-3993 or fax (317) 572-4002.

Wiley also publishes its books in a variety of electronic formats. Some content that appears in print may not be available in electronic books. For more information about Wiley products, visit our web site at www.wiley.com.

ISBN 13: 978-0-471-78274-2 (cloth)
ISBN 10: 0-471-78274-2 (cloth)

Printed in the United States of America.

10 9 8 7 6 5 4 3 2 1

To Mary,
my partner in love and life,
and to my parents,
Claude and Pat Pennington,
for setting an example.

Contents

Contents

Contents

Contents

Contents

Preface

Why is Wal-Mart the largest retailer in the world? Why are General Electric and Procter & Gamble perennial stars in the marketplace? On a personal level, what is it about your favorite restaurant, dry cleaner, or auto dealership that makes them stand out from the crowd?

It can't be just products, services, or price. There is competition everywhere—even for the government. And yet, there are businesses, government agencies, and nonprofit organizations that don't just compete with the others, they blow them away in areas like product and service quality, innovation, execution, and most important, results.

Your competitors don't hire all geniuses while you are left with the dunces. Their computer systems, compensation, and operational processes are not dramatically different from yours. When they sit around talking strategy, the words on their flip charts are not significantly more insightful than yours. The difference is, ultimately, an intangible that you need to know about.

Over the past 30 years I've worked for, consulted with, researched, and presented to organizations across a wide spectrum of industries and sectors. Along the way, I've noticed two things:

1. The best leaders, organizations, and individual contributors live by a mantra that can best be described as *Results Rule!* The goal is not the same for every organization. For some, it is profit. For others, it is service to a constituent group or staying within a budget. Whatever the business, the best ones never lose focus on the desired result.

2. *Results Rule!* organizations create and nurture a compelling culture that becomes their sustainable advantage. Every person operates from a sense of personal ownership and stewardship. Change in pursuit of the mission is embraced. Talented people appreciate the opportunity to come on board and contribute.

This book is about how to build a culture that sets your business apart from your competitors. Think of it as the intangibles that will allow your operation to be the standard by which your competitors are measured.

Becoming a *Results Rule!* organization means having confidence that you will execute efficiently and effectively, engage your associates and staff, and quickly respond to shifts in the marketplace. It doesn't matter if you aspire to be the low-cost provider or a high-end player, your competitive edge is ultimately a culture that delivers meaningful results.

Preface

At this point, you may be wondering why a book about achieving results? Isn't this, as Tom Peters said, "a blinding flash of the obvious?"

Consider this:

- We live in a "me too" world where products and services are commodities. Margins are being squeezed. And in this environment, the only ways to deliver results are to improve efficiencies to compete on price or become so valuable you command a premium. You are destined for a life of mediocrity (or worse) unless you grow an organization capable of delivering results year . . . after year . . . after year. We're talking about building a dynasty not having a single great season.
- Many organizations have a history of confusing tools and goals. It is the tendency to practice MBBS—Management by Best Seller—rather than do the hard work of executing day in and day out. This is not a slam against organizational initiatives. The vast majority are well intentioned and useful. But too often, the zeal to implement the latest new program clouds our ability to focus on results.
- There is a danger of confusing participation and activity with accomplishment. A friend told me about a conversation among parents about trophies to be given to each child for participating on a soccer team. When one parent questioned why such elaborate recognition was necessary for a team that finished last

in the league, the response was, "Fine. You explain to your child why she is the only one who didn't receive a trophy."

This was no isolated event. The generation entering today's workplace has a skill set and worldview enabling them to achieve amazing things. But, they have also been sheltered and made to feel special more than any generation in our history. Their life has been programmed, in many cases, to the point that a directive to "go outside and play" is met with a blank stare. Trophies and ribbons are awarded for everything because we want to promote self-esteem.

Organizations have a similar tendency. We reward ourselves and others for achieving performance measures with no connection to meaningful results.

Recognition is important, and there is no doubt people perform better when they feel good about themselves. But let's not confuse participation with accomplishment.

This book will introduce you to people and organizations who deliver results in today's world. The examples were chosen both from organizations with which I have worked and from organizations I have researched that consistently deliver results. They are designed to be representative rather than exhaustive.

You will see the familiar names of market leaders. It is virtually impossible to discuss the impact of culture and commitment to results without mentioning Southwest Airlines, Dell, Wal-Mart, and General Electric.

You will also meet individuals and organizations whose stories rarely, if ever, appear in the media. Smith-Bucklin is the largest association management company in the world. CreditSolutions.com is a hypergrowth company, and One Smooth Stone is an event marketing firm known for innovative work with many of the best-known companies in the United States. All three have made their culture the centerpiece on which success is built.

You will meet fun companies like Amy's Ice Cream and Mirror, and even a municipal government—the Town of Addison, Texas. There is a community bank with $800 million in assets; a second-generation family-owned manufacturing company that produces precision solid carbide rotary cutting tools; and the number-one Lexus dealership in the United States. You will even meet my friends at Cantina Laredo restaurants and discover why I'm there about 40 times per year.

Each of these organizations continues to develop its own unique culture to succeed in its own unique market-place. And despite the differences, there are similarities. I call them the *Six Choices.*

Results Rule! cultures choose to:

1. Tell themselves the truth and value candor and honesty.
2. Pursue the best over the easiest in every situation.
3. Leverage the power of partnerships both internally and externally.

4. Focus the energy to make the main things the main thing.
5. Show the courage of accountability.
6. Learn, grow, and improve every day.

Two themes consistently appear throughout this book:

1. Delivering results is more about what you do than what you know. The heroes of the marketplace minimize the gap between knowing and doing. The big difference is that *Results Rule!* organizations actually do this stuff in every part of their business—strategy development, operations, and people.
2. There is no 6-, 10-, or even 12-step plan for building a culture that sets you apart in the marketplace. Some of the strategies and tactics you see here can be applied immediately to your environment. Others can be adapted once the principle is embraced.

Chapter 1 makes the case that culture is your ultimate competitive edge. You will learn the characteristics of a *Results Rule!* culture and discover several ways to know your culture is in trouble.

Chapter 2 is about truth and candor. The reality is there are three types of organizations—has-beens, wannabes, and heroes. Nothing ever really changes until we tell ourselves the truth, and this chapter gives you a picture of where you stand.

Chapter 3 is one of the most important—choosing and pursuing the best over the easiest. Do you pursue the best strategy for delivering meaningful results, or do you take the easy road and follow your competitor? Do you make the best operational decisions, or do you cut corners to get the product out the door? Do you select the best people or are you willing to settle for the person who is immediately available even though qualifications and fit are marginal?

Chapter 4 is about leveraging the power of partnerships. Here's a hint: If your customers are not voluntarily selling for you, there is work to be done.

Chapter 5 deals with focusing the energy, and you will see how several organizations use their purpose, principles, goals, and processes to ensure they are delivering meaningful results.

Chapter 6 addresses accountability. It is one of the biggest problems for individuals and organizations. Once you master this one, it becomes a question of how to overcome challenges rather than will they be addressed.

Past success proves you were right once. Chapter 7 shares several ideas for maintaining a love affair with results by embracing change, learning, and growing to meet new demands.

Make this book your own. The concepts and ideas work if you are a company of one or one hundred thousand. Write in the margins, underline, highlight, and fold the corners of pages to remember the parts to which you want to refer back.

Preface

You can read this book in a relatively short period of time. You can study it forever. The chapters can be read consecutively or randomly.

You won't find a great deal of statistics or comparative analysis. Some might even find fault that this book shares more stories than theory or even statistics. My experience is stories, examples, and application are more likely to be read than charts. They are included if appropriate, but I acknowledge that much of this information is (from the purest perspective) anecdotal.

Albert Einstein once said: "Everything should be made as simple as possible, but not simpler."

My goal is to share ideas you can use immediately to create a *Results Rule!* business in a simple, straightforward (and hopefully entertaining) style.

Are you ready?

Let's get started.

RANDY PENNINGTON

January 2006

Acknowledgments

Every effort to expand knowledge, encourage thinking, and inspire action is a shared process. This one is no different. I wish to say thank you to the following individuals and organizations for encouraging and contributing to this project:

- Larry Winget and Joe Calloway gave me the push this project needed to get moving.
- Violet Cieri challenged me to think differently about what I do, and from a series of conversations, *Results Rule!* was born.
- My buddies in the business. You know who you are, and your friendship, example, and support mean the world to me.
- The leaders—individuals and organizations—with whom I have worked over the years have taught me more than I could ever imagine about building enduring organizations and delivering results. You will read about and hear from a few of them in this book, and I owe them a debt of gratitude for participating in this project.

Acknowledgments

- Matt Holt and the team at Wiley made this project enjoyable and fun. Special thanks goes to Shannon Vargo for your valuable feedback and assistance.
- The team at Publications Development Company made the book look great. Thank you for being patient and creative.
- Gary Rifkin supplied valuable input to help key points come alive.
- Beverly Gracia did a fabulous job helping me polish the manuscript.
- And finally to my wife, Mary. You gladly gave up weekends, evenings, and our personal time to make the space for this book to be completed. Most important, you have been my biggest fan, trusted business partner, and best friend through it all. How could anyone be any luckier than to find someone like you?

RESULTS RULE!

Chapter 1

It's the Culture, Stupid!

So my biggest concern is that somehow . . . we lose the espirit de corps, the culture, the spirit. If we ever do lose that, we will have lost our most valuable competitive asset.[1]

—Herb Kelleher, Chairman,
Southwest Airlines

❑ The Marketplace Speaks ❑

The marketplace never lies—*Results Rule!* It is the standard for measuring success if you are competing on the tennis court or in the district court; in the classroom or in the boardroom. And it applies to everyone at every level.

The second place team is never invited to hold the Super Bowl trophy and make the clichéd comments we hear every year. That honor goes to the team that delivered the results on the field. There are five nominees for the Academy Award for Best Picture each year, but only one movie producer is interrupted by the orchestra during the usually overlong acceptance speech.

1

Wal-Mart became a member of the exclusive club called the *Fortune 1* because of results. Dell was named *Fortune*'s Most Admired Company in 2005 because of—you guessed it—results.

Need more examples? How about these:

- *Toyota:* It is the gold—no make that platinum—standard for manufacturing automobiles of amazing quality in every price range built in some of the world's most efficient manufacturing plants year after year after year.
- *Nordstrom:* Lots of choices and knock-your-socks-off service in every store every time.
- *Wegmans Food Markets, Publix, and Whole Foods:* Three grocery store chains that prove knowledgeable, caring people can keep customers coming back over and over again. And, yes, they are making substantial profits in an industry where margins are measured in fractions.
- *The Container Store:* Enthusiastic people with a passion to help you organize (and simplify) your space and growing like crazy.
- *General Electric:* Over 100 years of technological leadership from a global company that continues to reinvent itself as a leader in sales, profits, and redefining how organizations operate.
- *Starbucks:* Because they enjoy the drinks, the environment, and the people, over 33 million people line

up each week to pay premium prices for a product you can make at home for pennies.

❏ What the Best Know and Do ❏

Organizations like these don't just succeed. They blow the competition away in terms of service, productivity, innovation, and execution. Their performance shouts *Results Rule!* Their competitive edge is a compelling culture that wins the hearts, minds, and loyalty of employees and customers.

That's it? How about products, services, strategies? Aren't they important differentiators?

Maybe, but it's doubtful.

Coffee, Corn, and You

The days when having a good product or service guaranteed you at least a minimum level of success are gone. Offering quality products or services has become the minimum requirement to enter and stay in the game.

Joe Calloway, author and authority on strategic branding, puts it this way: "The marketplace has become 'commoditized.' Customers see parity everywhere."[2]

Customers see parity because there is parity. Your competitors are only a telephone call or web site visit away from offering customers basically the same product and service features as you—for a similar or lower price.

3

And that means in the customer's eye we are all just like coffee, corn, and every other commodity traded on the open markets throughout the world. Our value to the customer is based solely on supply and demand.

But We Have a Better Strategy

Let's assume for a moment that your strategy is superior to your competitors'. How long will it take them to copy or improve on it? What guarantee do you have that market conditions won't change overnight and make your strategy obsolete or even detrimental to your success?

Even large organizations move at speeds unheard of just a few years ago.

Here is one example: General Electric moved its source for steel casings for turbines to Mexico because they were able to manufacture the casings there for 40 percent less than the cost of making them in the United States. Then they moved manufacturing from Mexico to Korea where they are able to make the casings for 40 percent less than in Mexico. The total time it took to move the operation from Mexico to Korea was *45 days*.

If one of the largest companies in the world can move that quickly to change its strategy and execution, can you really believe that whatever you are doing today is immune from becoming completely obsolete? Perhaps that is why former CEO Jack Welch noted, "All this crap you planned for is meaningless, basically. What's important is that you're agile, in your thinking and in your action."[3]

4

You may offer a unique product or service right now, but if what you are providing has value, sooner or later competition for your slice of the market will arise. The more people or companies there are who can compete with you, the closer you are to becoming an entirely "me too" business or profession defined by the similarities rather than the uniqueness of your offering. In an environment where everyone is doing the same things, culture beats strategy every time.

❏ 32 Years and Counting ❏

Three words come to mind when you ask people about Southwest Airlines—*fun, reliable,* and *inexpensive.* And they wouldn't have it any other way. Their mission is "dedication to the highest quality of Customer Service delivered with a sense of warmth, friendliness, individual pride, and company spirit."

The other word you should associate with Southwest is *profitable.* At the time of this writing, Southwest Airlines has delivered over 32 years of consistent quarterly profits in an industry where many players haven't had 32 *weeks* of consistent profit.

So what makes Southwest different?

People point to their route structure, low operating costs, no meal service, and the fact that they only fly one type of airplane, thereby saving on maintenance and training expense.

Those are certainly factors, but it doesn't explain why no one has been able to copy Southwest's success despite repeated attempts to replicate their strategy. The answer lies in the culture.

Chairman and former CEO Herb Kelleher said, "You can get airplanes, you can get ticket counter space, you can get tugs, you can get baggage conveyors. But the spirit of Southwest is the most difficult thing to emulate."[4]

Southwest knows that having a procedure stating airplanes will be turned in 20 minutes between trips is much less important than having a culture where it is expected and every employee takes meeting that expectation personally. The same can be said of their commitment to fun, service, and cost efficiency.

Does Your Culture Make a Financial Difference?

That is the question I posed to CEOs in a variety of industries. Their response was a unanimous, *Yes!*

SmithBucklin is the largest association management company in the world. Its clients include the Pet Food Institute, Society for Information Management, and National Association of Orthapedic Nurses. Henry Givray, who had previously worked at the company from 1983 to 1988, returned in 2002 as its president and CEO. Most CEOs work on strategy, sales, operational efficiencies, or the like. The first thing Henry worked on was the culture. He was so focused on the issue that several senior leaders wondered if he really knew what he was doing.

Henry put it this way, "I never heard people talking about organizational culture when I went to work in the 1980s. But over the years, I've concluded that if an authentic organizational culture that gives guidance and inspires can be articulated, aligned, reinforced, and preserved, it will mean the difference between having a good year and building an enduring company. So I made culture the first thing I worked on with the leadership team."

Realizing that several of you might write off Henry's statement as an example of corporate psychobabble, I asked him if he could quantify his love affair with culture. His response proves his point:

> In the 3 years since we began focusing on SmithBucklin culture, we've shattered every performance record from the previous 50 years. Growth, client acquisition, profitability, employee satisfaction—all of them.

Pretty impressive, huh?

Henry's comments were echoed by leaders in all types of industries. Gary Nelon, CEO of First Texas Bancorp said, "Our business model is people—rather than product—centric. We know that our culture promotes long-term relationships with our employees, our employees develop long-term relationships with the communities we serve, and we make more money."

It's Always Been That Way

Thomas Watson Jr., CEO of International Business Machines from 1956 to 1971, said, "the basic philosophy, spirit, and drive of an organization have far more to do with its relative achievements then do technological or economic resources, organizational structure, innovation, and timing."[5]

Those are strong words from the person who decided to launch a new line of mainframe computers in 1964 in a move *Fortune* magazine called "IBM's $5 Billion Gamble."[6] Watson's belief in the power of the IBM culture permeated the organization and contributed to the company's market dominance for generations.

Procter & Gamble (P&G), based on its more than 150 years of success, also qualifies as an organization that believes *Results Rule!* William Procter and John Gamble entered the highly competitive soap and candle industry in 1837. That might not sound like a growth industry now, but remember candles and soap were important products at that time. There were 14 other direct competitors in Cincinnati, Ohio, alone.

Many people know P&G as the creator of legendary brands such as Ivory Soap, Tide, and Crest. Some will recognize its leadership in marketing and market research. Harley Procter, William's son, was one of the first businessmen to experience success with display ads. The company founded its own market research group in 1924 and was a leading sponsor of the early soap opera.

Few people know, however, that William Cooper Procter, grandson of the founder, revised the company's articles of incorporation to read the "interests of the Company and its employees are inseparable."

Procter & Gamble's brands are legendary. My mother never sent me to the store to purchase laundry detergent. I was instructed to go pick up some Tide. She didn't cook with oil. She always cooked with Crisco. Today, my wife's grocery list will say "Ivory" and not bath soap. And while the company has always been an innovative and consistent advertiser, its reputation is built on performance.

The P&G culture is based on a defined purpose, set of values, and operating principles. The company is disciplined, customer focused, and proactive. Its values talk about a passion for winning, leadership at all levels, integrity, trust, and a sense of personal ownership.

I witnessed the P&G culture in action some years ago as a consultant working with the soap plant in St. Louis, Missouri, to design and implement a new employee discipline process. I had read about the company's focus on strategic thinking and fact-based decision making before beginning the project, but that did not prepare me for the way in which those principles were institutionalized in the culture.

The first time I answered a question with the words "I think," there was a slight and simultaneous grimace on the 12 or so faces on our design team. The second time I said "I think" it was challenged. And, fortunately, my key contact gave me some valuable advice at break. At P&G a better response is, "our experience shows," or "our statistics indicate."

Culture Is More than Feeling Good

I always feel a moment of apprehension when the person sitting next to me on an airplane asks, "So what do you do?" The anxiety increases exponentially when you are not seated on the aisle where you can make a fast getaway.

Nevertheless, I found myself in exactly that situation a few months back. I gave my standard response, "I help leaders and organizations create cultures focused on results."

My neighbor's response captured my attention: "Oh, we don't do that stuff."

I recognize a marketing opportunity as readily as the next person, and I inquired, "What parts of it don't you do?"

"Oh," the individual continued, "culture is about making everyone feel good, and being nice to people, and stuff like that. We don't do that stuff. We are all about the numbers."

So are the folks at P&G, and most people would agree that their culture is a vital part of their success. Tom Peters and Bob Waterman included P&G in their 1982 book, *In Search of Excellence.* James Collins and Jerry Porras highlighted P&G in their book *Built To Last.* You don't become an enduring company simply because you make people feel good. People's Express Airlines made people feel good, and it lasted only about 6 years.

Six years versus over 150 years. You do the math. You can't deliver results without a great culture, but a great culture without results has no value.

Your organization's culture is about much, much more than making people feel good. Engaging people is a big part of it, but engagement without execution is a recipe for extinction.

Everyone Has a Culture

I like the definition of culture from the *MSN Encarta Dictionary* as well as any I have seen: Culture is "the patterns of behavior and thinking that people living in social groups learn, create, and share."

An organization's culture includes its beliefs, expectations, rules of behavior, language, rituals, symbols, technology, styles of dress, ways of interacting, processes for communicating and maintaining power, and methods for reinforcing and modifying behavior and performance.

The guy sitting next to me on the airplane had it wrong—or at the very least not all correct. His company did have a culture, although you will not be seeing it listed by name as a positive example. Every organization has a culture that contributes to or detracts from its ability to deliver results in today's marketplace. Your objective is to determine the type of culture you need to deliver results.

❑ A *Results Rule!* Culture ❑

Results Rule! cultures are defined by the following:

- A set of organizational beliefs, assumptions, and values supporting a commitment to results, relationships both externally and internally, and accountability
- Consistent achievement of desired results that set the organization apart in the minds of customers, employees, and stakeholders

- People who do what they say they will do and make choices based on an attitude of stewardship and ownership
- Mutual respect, cooperation, and a high degree of trust between individuals and their managers, teams, and departments
- Alignment of individual, team, and departmental performance with the organization's strategic business objectives
- Continuous improvement and innovation—both large and small—at every level of the organization to improve effectiveness and efficiency
- An environment that attracts and retains top talent who value the opportunity to contribute

Your Culture Will Be Unique

The First Texas Bancorp culture is different from that of SmithBucklin. SmithBucklin's is different than that of P&G. And P&G's is different from that of Southwest Airlines.

For your culture to become your competitive edge, it must be based on your realities and decisions. It is doubtful you would see the CEO at P&G show up for Halloween dressed as a member of the 1970s rock group KISS. Yet, that is a perfect fit for Southwest Airlines CEO Gary Kelly.

It is the people in a company that make business work. Great strategies fail without a culture focused on and committed to delivering results that matter in your situation.

Terrence Deal and Allan Kennedy identified a number of elements determining an organization's culture in their book *Corporate Cultures: The Rites and Rituals of Corporate Life*.[7] They include the following:

- *Business environment*: Sales-driven organizations often have a different culture than research or service-driven groups.
- *Values*: The basic concepts and beliefs on which the organization is built. Some groups state them as dreams and aspirations. Others define them quite literally as the standards by which everyone operates.
- *Heroes*: These are the role models (sanctioned or nonsanctioned) that let people know what the organization really values. In the best organizations, heroes display the organization's stated values.
- *Rites and rituals*: The routines of daily life that provide visible and powerful messages about the way things really work.
- *Cultural network*: The communication network that carries the values, beliefs, assumptions, and expectations.

We Want to Be Them

"We want to be the Southwest Airlines of our industry."

I found the comment from this prospective client interesting and decided to dig a little deeper: "Why is that important to you?"

"Because if we have a culture like Southwest's, we will be able to perform like Southwest."

We all know what happened prior to this conversation. Someone read an article or attended a presentation about Southwest Airlines' wonderful culture. And this client's take-away lesson was that every problem would be solved if they could just instill that culture in their organization.

It is a tempting thought—get a new culture and watch performance improve and results shoot through the roof. Unfortunately, it doesn't work that way. Your organization's culture is not a piece of software that can be downloaded and launched. It must be guided, influenced, and reinforced over time.

❏ Organizational DNA ❏

Great, enduring organizations shout *Results Rule!* through their performance. It is part of their DNA. Not DNA in a biological sense, but DNA in a business sense. This DNA is learned and honed over time. DNA stands for Discipline, Nature, and Attitude.

Results Rule! organizations have the discipline to stay focused and execute flawlessly. They have a nature of stewardship, service, and integrity that leads to partnerships both internally and externally. Individuals in these organizations have an attitude of accountability and passion for achieving results that set them apart from those who merely talk a great game and then fail to deliver. They don't make excuses. They learn from mistakes and move on.

Just as human DNA automatically transmits an individual's genetic code—everything that individual is—to the next generation, business DNA transmits your message to the customer or client. The discipline, nature, and attitudes evident in your organization contribute to the overall culture—from the importance of honoring commitments to how customers and employees are treated.

Results Rule! organizations use this dynamic to their advantage. While technology, value chains, distribution models, and even strategic plans have their place, they are not what make an enduring organization. Positioning the culture of your organization as the DNA that drives results engages people and allows you to instill a level of commitment at every level. It enables you to be efficient, effective, and unique—to separate yourself from the competition.

Here's the difference between humans and organizations—organizations can choose to change their genetic makeup. It's not easy, and it takes a while. But it can be done.

❑ Change Performance to Change the Culture ❑

I have read many purpose and values statements while working with different organizations. Not a single one of them says, "We exist to alienate our customers and abuse our employees." But that is what often happens in real life. And like the prospect mentioned earlier in this chapter, there is a wish to change the culture as a means to improving the performance. Leaders and organizations with this mind-set have it backward. *You change the performance to change the culture.*

Assumptions, beliefs, and values drive behavior and performance. Performance and behavior demonstrated over time become habit. And habits define the culture of your organization.

To build a *Results Rule!* culture, you must first build the habits that make you perform and behave like the purpose and values you hang on the wall.

❏ Is Your Culture in Trouble? ❏

I have always appreciated comedian Jeff Foxworthy's, "You know you are a redneck if . . ." bits. This model can easily be applied to an organization's culture: You know your culture is the factor limiting your results if you see:

- *High turnover and low morale:* Good employees decide to pursue other opportunities. Individuals remaining with the organization become demoralized and lethargic in the performance of their duties.
- *On-going inconsistency:* Everyone has an off-day occasionally. Performance that continually gyrates all over the map is a reflection on the culture. Consistency is one mark of a *Results Rule!* organization.
- *Lack of focus on the external environment:* Cultures in distress look internally at all the things that are going

wrong. *Results Rule!* cultures focus on serving the customer. They compete against others in the marketplace rather than against themselves.

- *Short-term thinking:* Survival in today's competitive marketplace requires constant attention to results. That, however, should not be an excuse for short-term thinking. *Results Rule!* cultures refuse to sacrifice long-term viability for short-term success. They look for both.
- *Rise of destructive subcultures:* Pride in one's team is admirable. Allowing team pride to deteriorate into impenetrable organizational silos is a sure sign of a fractured culture.
- *Undermining the success of others:* Disagreements that turn into vendettas. Information purposely withheld. These are the symptoms of a culture where team is considered a four-letter word.
- *Increased cynicism:* Cultures that are in trouble look at all change—good or bad—through cynical eyes that assume the worst possible outcome. *Results Rule!* cultures take a critical look at opportunities to improve and embrace those that offer a satisfactory return on investment and energy.

❏ It's Never Just One Thing ❏

Building a culture that blows the competition away is a little like making a really great sauce. Admittedly, I don't make a great sauce. In fact, for me, cooking usually

17

involves mixing salad ingredients or (more likely) using a microwave oven.

My wife, on the other hand, is an amazing cook who makes incredible sauces. Over the years, I've learned to appreciate the art, science, and dedication of her expertise. When I ask her for the three, five, or even seven steps to making the perfect sauce, she just laughs.

She will spend hours simmering, reducing, and adding just the right mix of ingredients to create a unique masterpiece. And the next time out, she will try to improve it.

Leaders who create a compelling culture do basically the same thing. I have identified, through research and over 20 years of field experience, six things *Results Rule!* organizations do differently and/or more often than their competitors. Think of them as the *six choices* that distinguish enduring organizations from their competitors. The chapters to follow address each of them in more detail.

Results Rule! cultures choose to:

1. Tell themselves the truth and value candor and honesty.
2. Pursue the best over the easiest in every situation.
3. Leverage the power of partnerships both internally and externally.
4. Focus the energy to make the main things the main thing.

5. Show the courage of accountability.
6. Learn, grow, and improve every day.

There is no one correct formula. The ingredients are mixed differently in each situation. Some strategies even address multiple areas. It's never just one thing.

❏ Everyone Leads ❏

Most leadership development programs miss the point. The actual program is okay, it's just that the target audience is too limited. We assume that the leaders are those with the term *manager* or *supervisor* in their job description and only those people are responsible for the creation of the culture. What a terrible waste.

Leadership is the art of influencing the actions and outcomes of others to deliver results. Using that definition, anyone can be and everyone is a leader. In my experience, some of the most influential people in an organization have titles such as administrative assistant, maintenance mechanic, computer systems analyst, or customer service representative.

Sure, managers and human resources personnel play an important role, but a nonmanager talking about how "everything is screwed up around here" has just as much, if not more, impact as anything said or done by *management.*

Your organization's culture determines how things are done regardless of any policy, directive, or management initiative. Experience tells me that there are things going on in your organization about which the people in charge have no clue. If you don't believe me, have an open conversation with your receptionist or the senior administrative assistant in your office. You will likely learn a great deal about how things are really done at your place of business.

Results Rule! organizations refuse to accept that only the "Suits" or Human Resources have responsibility for creating and maintaining the culture. It is everyone's responsibility because we all create the culture.

RESULTS RULES

- A compelling culture is your competitive edge in a world where products and services are commodities.
- Every organization has a culture that contributes to or detracts from its ability to deliver results in today's marketplace. Your objective is to determine the type of culture you need to deliver results.
- Enduring organizations shout *Results Rule!* through their performance. It is part of their business DNA— Discipline, Nature, and Attitude.
- If you wait for the culture to change before your performance changes, nothing will ever happen. Culture change follows performance change, not the other way around.

- There is no magic formula for creating a compelling culture. The ingredients are the same, but they are mixed differently in each situation. The challenge is to find the mix that sets you apart.
- Everyone influences someone. It is your responsibility to contribute to the culture.

Chapter 2

Has-Beens, Wannabes, and Heroes

The truth shall set you free. But first, it will tick you off.[1]

—Larry Winget

In the mind of your customer you are either a has-been, a wannabe, or a hero. They, not you, determine whether or not you stand out from the crowd. They let you know if your culture is working for you or against you.

So what type of organization do you work in?

Take an honest look at your results. Not just last quarter's profit and loss statement or sales numbers. Look at all the overall results. How satisfied are your customers? Are your margins comparable to (or better than) your competitors? Are employee turnover rates or low satisfaction ratings dragging down performance? How is your cash flow? Are you living your values? Are your dreams and aspirations coming true?

Don't stop at this year's results. Look at last year, and the year before, and the year before that. A single great year does not necessarily make you a marketplace hero. Maybe you were simply lucky.

❏ **You Know Them by Their Performance** ❏

It doesn't take much to be a has-been. While offering un-remarkable products and services places you on the fast track, a slower route to obscurity is to continue doing what you've always done—especially if it was successful at some point—and wait for the world to pass you by.

Has-beens can survive for long periods. In fact, some eke out an existence for years either blissfully out of touch with reality, resigned to mediocre results, or maintained on life support through artificial means.

It takes more effort to be a wannabe. Wannabes can look like heroes at first glance much the way a cubic zirconium can look like a diamond. Both sparkle from a distance, but the difference becomes obvious on closer inspection.

Wannabes say all the right things. They have a mission and a vision, and their values statements are posted on their walls. They implement the latest management programs, convinced that the next one will put them over the top. They just can't, or won't, produce consistent results.

Some wannabes are en route to being heroes; they simply need a little seasoning and experience to make the leap. Most never make the transition. They are, to coin an old Texas phrase, all hat and no cattle. There is no steak to go along with the sizzle.

❏ The Two-Year Wonders ❏

I spent several years with a boutique consulting firm. By every outward appearance, we were marketplace heroes with a client list including seven of the *Fortune* 10, great margins, and a talented staff.

The problem was inconsistency. We experienced incredible growth followed by a period of slashing salaries, and sometimes laying off employees, just to stay afloat. You could explain it away by saying that the company was the victim of an economic downturn if it happened once. A pattern repeating itself on a two-year cycle suggests we were not telling ourselves the truth about our business.

In short, we were wannabes. We assumed a couple of winning seasons automatically translated into a dynasty. It doesn't happen that way, and it took a couple of painful experiences to learn this critical lesson.

❏ Are You on the Right Track? ❏

Do you have the makings of a marketplace hero? Does your performance and the performance of your organization shout out *Results Rule?*

Table 2.1 provides a quick quiz to give you an idea where your organization falls in this spectrum. It's not scientific, but it will give you a snapshot of where you are.

Table 2.1   *Results Rule!* Quiz

Rate yourself from 1 to 5 using the following scale:

5 = Look in the dictionary and you will see our picture as an example.

4 = It is the exception rather than the rule when this doesn't happen.

3 = We make a consistent effort and do okay about half the time.

2 = Occasionally, but it is probably by accident.

1 = What are you—high?

	1	2	3	4	5
A common set of beliefs, assumptions, and values drive a commitment to results, relationships, and accountability. There is a consistency of purpose.					
Leaders at every level consistently model specific behaviors, attitudes, and skills that produce long-term voluntary commitment across the enterprise.					
People take their performance personally. A sense of ownership and personal responsibility exists at every level.					
Mutual respect, cooperation, and a high degree of trust exist between individuals, teams, and departments. to the opinions of others.					

Table 2.1   Continued

	1	2	3	4	5
Goals at every level of the organization are aligned and focused to deliver excellence that helps us stand out in the marketplace.					
Customers love us so much they voluntarily sell for us.					
The opportunity to work here attracts quality talent and retains top performers who appreciate the opportunity to succeed.					
Everyone views change as a positive tool to continuously improve our performance and adapt to new demands and opportunties.					
Integrity is the code by which we live and die.					
A high degree of candor and open communication exists. People at every level are comfortable saying what needs to be said and listening to the opinions of others.					

Scoring:

- *If you scored a 50:* You either work for one of the best companies on the planet, or you may need to be more honest in

(continued)

Table 2.1   Continued

your assessment. If you do work for an extraordinary company, congratulations. We would like to hear from you.

- *If you scored between 40 and 50:* You are definitely on the road to being a hero. Keep at it, and realize that the last few steps will be the most difficult.
- *If you scored between 30 and 40:* You are a wannabe moving in the right direction. Taking it to the next level has the potential to set you apart in your marketplace.
- *If you scored below 30:* Thank you for telling the truth. If your score didn't bother you, you are probably on the road to has-been status. If it frustrates you, you are in the wannabe class. The good news is that you have taken an important step in becoming a marketplace hero and delivering consistent results.

The survey is included here—rather than in the previous chapter—because your culture will never change until you tell yourself the truth about your current state. As you might expect, the validity of the assessment is in direct proportion to your willingness to tell yourself the truth.

Faulty Thinking— Faulty Assumptions

Despite poor service, lousy product quality, and every other form of evidence to the contrary, very few organizations make a conscious decision to drive themselves out of business. So why are there so many has-beens and wannabes in the world?

Has-beens and wannabes often operate with 3-D vision—Denial, Distortion, and Delusion. They deny marketplace realities; distort their performance; and delude themselves into blaming their lousy results on everyone but themselves. It is part of their culture.

Organizations with 3-D vision make assumptions that doom them to something less than the hero status to which they aspire. Here are a few examples:

- *A branding campaign will solve all my problems.* A November 7, 2000, article on CNET News described the shutdown of Pets.com. This is what Troy Wolverton wrote: "The Amazon.com-backed company was the leading online pet store and was known for its wildly popular sock puppet spokesdog."[2]

The sock puppet? That's what it was known for? Not the quality of its service, the strength of its business model, or the execution of its strategy? No wonder you can still purchase the Pets.com sock puppet on eBay for $7.99, but you can no longer shop at Pets.com.

Great brands begin as great companies. Assuming success is the product of a branding campaign is a quick path to extinction. Remember, Noah built the ark before he prayed for rain.[3]

- *Technology will solve all my problems.* A study conducted by NFI Research stated, "Almost two-thirds of executives and managers today see information technology (IT) as the department that will provide their organizations with the most strategic competitive advantage two years from now."[4]

Huh?

Technology is a driving force for improving productivity. And the chances are good your organization will benefit from enhancements. But how can something everyone is investing in be anyone's most strategic competitive advantage?

- *A new strategic initiative will solve all my problems.* It is a Pavlovian response—a new solution is touted in the business press and the organization jumps into action with a new program to ensure:
  - Survival
  - Market dominance
  - Increased profitability, customer satisfaction, or morale
  - All of the above

Executives set the direction, resources are applied (often from the last uncompleted initiative), and employees are asked to jump through hoops again. Meanwhile, they are thinking, "This too shall pass."

- *Customer retention will solve all my problems.* You have heard the statistic in presentation after presentation—a 5 percent retention in customers will increase profits by 25 percent to 85 percent and it costs five times more to acquire a new customer than to re-tain a current one. Depending on your business, however, these statistics are not necessarily true.

Timothy Keiningham, Terry Vabra, Lezran Aksoy, and Henri Wallard poke significant holes in the premise that customer retention will solve all of your company's problems in their book *Loyalty Myths.*[5] The authors make the case that the connection between retention and profits depends on the organization's current retention rate, the current size of the profit percentage, and the profitability of the customers being retained. They sug-gest that 10 percent to 20 percent of most customers ac-tually lose money for the company. Retaining this group is not a plan for success. Volume losses are still losses.

Likewise, the authors suggest that many organizations actually miscalculate customer acquisition costs because they consider their marketing efforts to be solely for the purpose of increasing their customer base. However, marketing must still take place to maintain brand aware-ness among existing customers. In some industries, it ac-tually costs more to meet the expectations of highly profitable customers than to acquire a customer with lower expectations.

Are you noticing a trend? There is a potential truth in each assumption. And there is opportunity for an equally damaging consequence. *Results Rule!* cultures seek the truth based on their specific situation rather than relying on generalities.

❑ More Faulty Assumptions ❑

The list of faulty assumptions inspired by 3-D vision is endless. Here are a few others you may have encountered:

- *Customer complaints are a pain.* Yes, they can be challenging, but they are also your best source of information on how to improve your product or service. A study by the American Society for Quality and the Quality and Productivity Center showed that 82 percent of the customers who leave your business do so because of dissatisfaction with your product or an attitude of indifference on the part of the service provider. Would you prefer they did not tell you and just left?
- *The leader has to know all the answers.* No one wants their leader to be clueless, and no one expects the leader to be a master of every function. Max DePree, former CEO at Herman Miller said it well: "The first responsibility of a leader is to define reality. The last is to say thank you. In between the two, the leader must become a servant and a debtor."[6]
- *Low cost is the only way to go.* An Internet search for the word *discount* yielded 77,900,000 results. A search of the phrase *low cost* turned up 27,400,000 potential web sites to visit. Tires, books, car rentals, travel, shoes, printing, office supplies, you name it and the chances are excellent you can find someone to sell it to you at a discount. Wal-Mart, Dell, and Southwest Airlines are legendary for their ability to dominate the low-

cost marketplace. On the other hand, many hero companies have found sustainable success by avoiding the low-cost strategy. Tell yourself the truth about your product or service. If you exist in a commodity space, your culture must allow you to succeed there. But, don't assume that is the case. Look at your own buying habits. Do you make every purchase solely on the basis of price?

• *Employees only care about themselves:* Really? So why did the employees of Southwest Airlines volunteer to cut the grass at the corporate headquarters after 9/11? Employees do care about themselves. Who can blame them considering the changes in employee-employer relationships? But employees also care about the organization for which they work if given a reason to do so.

• *I know who my competition is.* Apple Computer was started by two kids in a garage. Dell Computer got its start in a dorm room at the University of Texas. Microsoft—a similar story. Who would have thought that the competition for an accounting position in the United States is a person sitting at a computer in Bangalore, India? You may have identified the usual suspects, but never forget that someone you never imagined is thinking about a way to dramatically change the face of your industry and your life.

• *The only things that matter are the bottom line numbers.* This one is tricky. It is also the place where heroes distinguish themselves.

Doug Van Arsdale, CEO of CreditSolutions.com, told me, "Every day I focus on results. Every day I look at the numbers."

Has-beens and wannabes point to such statements as a reason to focus on the bottom line to the exclusion of anything else. Heroes, like Van Arsdale, know that focusing solely on the numbers to the exclusion of more qualitative metrics tied to the culture he wants to create is a recipe for long-term mediocrity. Organizations living by the *Results Rule!* mantra maintain a dual focus on the qualitative and quantitative measures that deliver consistent results. Their continuous focus on results is matched only by their intense commitment to maintaining a unique and compelling culture.

❏ Moving toward Hero Status ❏

The cure for 3-D vision and the first step toward building a culture that blows the competition away is the continuous search for and acknowledgment of the truth.

Sounds easy doesn't it? The words just roll off the tongue. It is a platitude to which we can all nod our heads in agreement knowing that it rarely happens. Larry Bossidy and Ram Charan wrote, "Though businesspeople like to think of themselves as realists, the fact is that wishful thinking, denial, and other forms of avoiding reality are deeply embedded in most corporate cultures."[7]

❑   The Pressure to Avoid the Truth   ❑

Many have speculated how a well-respected firm such as Arthur Andersen could allow itself to be drawn into Enron's destructive deceptions. Didn't they know the truth about what was going on? Wouldn't they want to protect themselves and their client?

It turns out that at least some did know what was going on. They just didn't bother to let the Enron board of directors in on it.

Fourteen senior partners at Arthur Andersen met on February 5, 2001, to discuss whether Enron should be maintained as a client. Reports indicate that the Andersen leaders in attendance called Enron's use of mark-to-market accounting "intelligent gambling" and were concerned over "Enron's dependence on transaction execution to meet financial objectives."

A supposed outcome of the meeting was a decision to tell Enron's board to establish a committee for ensuring the fairness of its transactions with the private equity fund operated by its CFO.

The message was never conveyed.[8]

So why did the partners at Arthur Andersen avoid acknowledging the truth to themselves and telling it to the Enron board? What could generate that much pressure to avoid speaking out?

How about $52 million per year in revenue with the prospects of even more in the future?

There is a risk and reward for telling the truth in every organization. For Andersen, the potential risk was apparently outweighed by the opportunity for a huge financial reward. The partners were focused on results, just not the ones that would have allowed the company to survive.

❏ The Courage to Keep Asking ❏

Here's the situation: You have utilized a nationally known employee satisfaction survey for a number of years. Responses from your staff rank you in the top 20 percent nationally on every question. And yet, your employee turnover is twice the average of others in your industry and area.

Would you assume the real issue is low compensation and throw more money at the problem? Would you conclude that your staff is different from others and decide employee satisfaction surveys are of little use? Or would you go to your board, admit you were not sure what the problem is, and propose a plan to keep digging until the right questions and real answers could be identified?

Dr. Jim Hawkins, one of the most committed and forward-thinking public school superintendents I have met, chose to keep asking the question. Through a series of focus groups with over 20 percent of his faculty, he found that student behavior, not salary or job satisfaction, was the most important factor in teacher retention. As a result, he was able to focus his efforts on systemic solutions that mattered to all of his constituents rather than make a faulty assumption.

Remember, there is both a risk and a reward for telling the truth. The reward is obvious: Identifying and correcting the cause of high teacher turnover would make Dr. Hawkins and his team a hero. The potential for coming back with an answer that is not politically palatable to his board, however, could make him a has-been. Would you put your job on the line to ensure your organization knew the truth?

Dr. Hawkins demonstrated the courage to ask the difficult question. The leaders at Arthur Andersen didn't. It has nothing to do with your organization's size, revenue, or status. It is all about a culture that acknowledges reality and values the truth.

❏ The Truth Begins with ❏ Open Communication

In Wal-Mart's early days, Sam Walton began gathering with store managers on Saturday mornings to discuss merchandising. Those in attendance would critique the company's performance, plan promotions, and discuss items the company intended to purchase.[9]

Today, the Saturday Morning Meeting is the focal point for the company's communication strategy. Sam Walton believed this meeting was at the "very heart of the Wal-Mart culture."[10] Managers and associates from the corporate office attend as do associates from the field who are being recognized for excellent performance. Discussion topics range from what is selling in the stores to weaknesses identified to competitor performance — and yes, to how Wal-Mart will maintain its unique and competitive culture. Every topic is open for discussion and information discussed on Saturday mornings makes its way to stores by Monday morning.

Visitors (such as dignitaries, professional athletes, executives from supplier companies, and even celebrities) occasionally attend as well. Coleman Peterson, retired executive vice president of the People Division at Wal-Mart, told me the visitors in attendance often comment on "how articulate Wal-Mart people are." He believes people are really noticing how comfortable Wal-Mart associates are talking about business and personal issues in an open environment. Their comfort in communicating openly allows more meaningful discussion to take place.

"We are very candid with each other," Peterson says. "I believe one reason is we are very familiar with each other. Sam Walton loved to visit stores, and Wal-Mart executives spend, on average, three days per week in the field. That familiarity makes it easier to be open about everything. There aren't a lot of barriers between people at different levels of the organization."

❏ The Open Door ❏

The notion of having an open-door policy in place so that anyone is able to raise any issue has become almost clichéd in organizational life. I've encountered several individuals who have even physically removed their door to prove to the world they are committed to open communication.

What leader is going to say, "No, you can't talk to me?" What organization is going to distribute a policy stating, "Customer complaints are a waste of time, and we are not going to accept them?"

The true test of your commitment to open communication is not the absence of a door on your office or even sharing your e-mail address with your customers. It is people walking through the door (literally or virtually) to discuss what's on their minds and you having the commitment to listen.

❏ Selling Hats to Each Other ❏

Heroes actively seek and embrace the truth. Has-beens and wannabes avoid it.

Arriving as the CEO of Allied Signal, Larry Bossidy found a company that on the surface looked like the place from which he had come — General Electric. There were strategies, operating plans, and people processes. There were budgets and reviews. Unlike General Electric, however, none of these were producing desired levels of results. Bossidy said, "When you manage these processes in depth, you get robust outputs. You get answers to critical questions. At Allied Signal, we weren't even asking those questions. The processes were empty rituals."[11]

It is easy to understand Bossidy's frustration. His former boss at General Electric, Jack Welch, was noted for valuing the truth and looking at reality. Welch said, "An awful lot of ritual goes on in companies. A lot of what I call 'selling hats to each other.' "[12]

Selling hats to each other occurs any time you allow ritual to take precedent over substance. Do your budget and operational reviews focus on activities to the exclusion of results? How about your performance appraisal process? Do employees receive great ratings while the organization is delivering mediocre results? If so, you just bought or sold another shipment of hats.

Don't forget strategic planning. Are the strengths you are listing in the strengths, weaknesses, opportunities, and threats (SWOT) analysis really strengths? Do they set you apart from your competitors?

How about your talent? Is it as developed as you think it is?

The opportunities for selling hats are endless.

❏ You Can't Be All Three ❏

Here's an interesting exercise for your next staff meeting or leadership retreat. Pose this question and see what happens: "In the minds of the customers we serve, are we a has-been, wannabe, or hero organization?"

One client broke its 40+ senior leaders into small groups to tackle this question. Each group debated the pros and cons of each position for almost an hour and then reported their decision to the collective body. A few admitted that they were most likely wannabes. Most of the group, however, said there were elements of all three in their organization.

What happened next was a beautiful thing.

Just as the final small group report was rationalizing its way to selling another shipment of hats, the CEO jumped out of his seat and said, "If you ask me, we are a bunch of has-beens. We are just too scared to admit it."

The CEO went on to explain that if any part of the organization is a has-been, the entire organization is a has-been. Like shipmates on the same ocean liner, we share common disaster as well as common good. If the bow sails safely into the harbor, the stern arrives as well. If the bow sinks, the stern follows.

This leader made a tremendous stride in transforming his organization into a hero with one important realization: Everyone's future is intertwined.

❏ So What? ❏

Why should you care if the organization for which you work is a has-been, a wannabe, or a hero organization? What does it matter if you tell yourself the truth?

If you are the owner or a senior manager, the answer is obvious. That is basically your job, isn't it?

But how about if you are not one of the people who develop strategy, determine resources, or direct the actions of others. Why should you care?

I had the opportunity to implement one of those dreaded "strategic initiatives" with a wholesale grocery client a few years ago. The purpose was to improve working relationships, increase accountability, and focus everyone on desired results.

During a communication session with about 200 employees on the second shift, one person took the opportunity to let me know exactly what he thought.

"This is all bullshit!" he yelled from the back of the room.

Of all the things that came to mind as a response, I fortunately chose an appropriate one: "Excuse me?"

"You heard me. This is all bullshit!"

All eyes—including the managers huddling in the corner—were now focused on the two of us, and I decided to play this out.

"That's interesting. Why do you think that?" I responded. The answer floored me.

"You don't know our managers. They will never be able to pull this off."

I decided to tell it to him straight. "That's interesting because your managers said the same thing about you. So it seems you have a choice. You can decide to do what it takes to make this work, or two years from now there will be 20 percent fewer of you in this room."

The prediction was easy to make, and I wasn't surprised when it came true. I simply looked at their results. Margins were being squeezed. Competitors were encroaching on their customer base. And, everyone from the plant manager on down was caught in a self-fulfilling prophecy loop of mistrust and cynicism. They were on the fast track to has-been status and no one was willing to admit it.

❏ Results and Responsibility ❏

Heroes know they are promised only the opportunity to prove their worth in the marketplace. It is not about winning at all costs or some "greed is good" mind-set. We've seen the payoff from that type of thinking before. Do we really need to be reminded of the destruction that took place when individuals and organizations decided to divorce results from responsibility and accountability?

Heroes love the fact that *Results Rule!* And, they relish the opportunity to set themselves apart from the other guys by competing responsibly and ethically. It's a matter of passion, pride, and in today's world, survival.

❏ Can You Handle the Truth? ❏

Jack Nicholson played Colonel Nathan R. Jessep in the 1992 movie *A Few Good Men*. In the climactic scene, he is confronted by Lt. Daniel Kaffee (played by Tom Cruise) about what really happened in the murder case being investigated. As Kaffee pushes Jessep for the truth, Jessep gives the immortal line, "You want the truth? You can't handle the truth."

Can you handle the truth? *Results Rule!* organizations look for every opportunity to understand the reality of their strategies, operations, environments, and customers' experiences.

The marketplace never lies so why not tell yourself the truth. Nothing ever really changes until you do. Are you a has-been, wannabe, or hero?

RESULTS RULES

- You are either a has-been, a wannabe, or a hero in the mind of your customer. Marketplace heroes shout *Results Rule!* with their performance.
- Being a *Results Rule!* organization is not about winning at all costs. Marketplace heroes know you can't divorce the drive for results from the responsibility to act ethically if the goal is long-term success.
- Has-beens and wannabes are often guilty of 3-D vision—Denial, Distortion, and Delusion. They deny marketplace realities. They distort their performance; and they delude themselves into blaming their lousy results on everyone but themselves.

  The cure for 3-D vision and the first step toward being a marketplace hero is the continuous search for and acknowledgment of the truth.
- The true test of your commitment to open communication is not the absence of a door on your office or even sharing your e-mail with your customers. It is

people walking through the door (literally or virtually) to discuss what's on their minds and you having
the commitment to listen.

- Nothing ever really changes until you tell yourself
the truth.

Chapter 3

Pursue the Best over the Easiest

Truth is all around you. What matters is where you put your focus.[1]

—Roger von Oech, PhD

The *Results Rule!* organizations I've studied live by three rules:

1. Know who you are.
2. Know what you want to accomplish and how you want to accomplish it.
3. Focus all your energy on consistently meeting rules one and two.

These organizations utilize a variety of tools to turn their intentions into action: strategic plans; customer relationship management; outsourcing solutions; quality programs; activity-based management; balanced scorecards; and mission, vision, and value statements.

Then again, wannabe (and occasionally has-been) organizations do the same thing. Mission, vision, and value statements adorn the walls and cubicles of some of the worst companies in business.

The difference between *Results Rule!* organizations and the others often comes down to the choices they pursue.

❑ The Most Important ❑ Decision You Will Make

Sewell Automotive Companies operates highly successful auto dealerships. Its Cadillac and Lexus operations are perennially ranked at or near the top in the United States.

The Sewell dealerships know who they are: an automotive company. They know what they want to accomplish: to provide the best sales and service experience. They know how they want to accomplish it: through continuous improvement to become a top-performing, thoroughly professional, and genuinely caring organization.

Carl Sewell, the company's owner, says the choice to be the best was the most important decision his company ever made. Doing so made "life simpler, more fun, and definitely more profitable."[2] Here's what he means:

- Decisions become much easier when you have a clear standard against which to evaluate your choices. If a course of action will move you farther in your quest to be the best, you do it. If not, you don't.

- Achieving results makes everyone happier and that usually leads to even better performance. If you are someone who isn't energized by the opportunity to be the best, you will probably self-select out of the organization.
- Customers want to associate with successful companies. Given the choice, they will return to companies with a reputation for being the best at what they do.

❏   Three Types of Choices   ❏

The major decisions most organizations are faced with can be divided into three categories:

1. *The leadership component:* This includes all decisions regarding the organization's direction and performance:
   - Mission, vision, and values
   - Resource allocation
   - Strategic goals
   - Measurement and analysis of performance
   - Operational goals
   - Performance management
2. *The operational component:* This includes all decisions regarding the delivery of the organization's products and services including:
   - Product and service delivery
   - Information systems

- Customer engagement
- Support processes
3. *The people component:* This includes all decisions regarding hiring and retaining the right people in the right place at the right time and with the right attitude and motivation:
   - Selection
   - Work systems
   - Employee satisfaction
   - Employee education and training

The power of pursuing the best over the easiest to transform your organization is fully realized when it is applied in all three categories. This chapter provides examples of how it is being done in a number of successful companies.

❏ Pursuing Your Best Purpose ❏

Pursuing the best over the easiest in the leadership component of your organization is about more than articulating a mission, vision, or values statement to hang on the wall. It requires having both the personal and organizational discipline to hold every action and decision to a higher standard. Some *Results Rule!* organizations don't even have a formal mission statement. Or if they do, they don't call it that because of the bad experiences management and employees have had with statements in other organizations.

The husband and wife chef/owner team of Michael DeGregory and Colleen Belloise-DeGregory started a restaurant called Mirror in partnership with Joe Calloway (the author of the book quoted in Chapter 1). They have created a business that delivers results visit . . . after visit . . . after visit.

American Airlines in-flight magazine has named Mirror one of the hottest spots in America. Located in the revitalized 12th Street district of Nashville, Tennessee, this restaurant and bar is home to great food and the best martini in town (maybe the country).

Calloway told me, "We wanted a unique place that made customers feel like they weren't in Nashville any more. We used words like hip, imaginative, always great food, and welcoming. I've never been a huge fan of mission statements per se so there is nothing really formal written. Interestingly enough, almost all of the reviews have used the word hip, and many of them have said precisely that Mirror doesn't feel like a Nashville restaurant."

You see, it's not about the statement, it is about the choice and the discipline to pursue it.

❏ The Ticket to the Party ❏

When I was young, choosing the best automobile meant buying a Cadillac. Other luxury autos might have existed, but in my part of the world Cadillac was the standard. The name was so synonymous with purchasing the best we used Cadillac as an adjective. Schwinn made the Cadillac of bicycles. International Harvester made the Cadillac of tractors. And Dairy Queen made the Cadillac of ice cream sundaes.

There is no longer just one automobile manufacturer that has cornered the market on prestige. Cadillac might be on your list, but it would be joined by Lexus, Mercedes-Benz, Infiniti, and others. It is no different in the midpriced or economy markets.

Want leather seats? If one manufacturer offers them, they all do. It's the same with front-wheel (or all-wheel) drive, upgraded sound systems, chrome wheels, sun roofs, and cruise control. Everyone sells basically the same features for a similar price and payment terms. And each of them is basically equivalent in quality.

It is likely that the position of your product or service within your industry is very similar to this. A tax return is a tax return is a tax return. So are banking transactions, basic groceries, and virtually any of the products or services you use every day. There are over 1,000 types of shampoo. Do you think one really cleans your hair any better than another?

So why are you still assuming that simply delivering a fundamental feature is a big deal?

Pursuing the best over the easiest in today's world means realizing that successfully providing fundamentals is the minimum requirement for survival. Being distinctive determines success.

❑ Poor Fundamentals Make ❑ Your Distinction Irrelevant

This point was brought home in a two-day seminar I conducted for leaders in the financial services industry. On the first day, we discussed the idea that fundamentals are the minimum requirement and being distinctive is what determines success. At the beginning of the second day, one of the participants came in with the following story:

> We had heard about this seafood restaurant (name withheld on purpose) with great food and a really fun atmosphere so we decided to try it out last night. The meal I ordered was good, but the waiter didn't bring all of it at the same time. And, we had a terrible time getting anyone to serve us more drinks. The staff was having too much fun standing on tables singing and dancing. We had heard that the place was fun, but the fun things they did were irrelevant, and we'll never go back because they didn't get the fundamentals right.

I love what Joe Calloway told me. "The core of the offering at Mirror is the food. If the food—the core product—isn't great, we go out of business."

Notice that he didn't say, "If we deliver a great core product, people will beat down our door." He's too smart for that. In the market where he plays, great food is the fundamental element. The distinction is the hip atmosphere and great martinis.

If you fail to deliver on their fundamental expectations, you will lose customers. If you assume that just doing the fundamentals is enough, you will lose them as well. You cannot be a marketplace hero unless you build a culture in which everyone chooses to go beyond the basics to deliver something that makes you distinctive.

A Qualifier

There is a big difference between being distinctive and being weird. People remember different. They pay for distinctive. It is easy to be different. Being distinctive takes discipline and hard work to ensure value is added.

❑ If the Government Can ❑
Do It, Why Can't You?

I spoke with Paula Julian, senior vice president of brand planning at Rapp Collins Worldwide, about the idea that providing the fundamental elements is the minimum requirement and being distinctive makes the difference that will lead to success in today's marketplace. Her experience has been that many organizations shoot themselves in the foot by either confusing basic expectations with something unique or, even worse, assuming they have nothing really different to offer. According to Paula, "Companies that fall into that trap are just not thinking hard enough."

So if you believe you are unable to deliver both the fundamental elements and achieve distinction, consider this: There is a municipal government in Texas that has figured it out, and if a government agency responsible for a city with a daytime population of 100,000 that can deliver both, so can you.

The Town of Addison, Texas, is a 4.5-square-mile suburb of Dallas. The fundamentals in municipal government include streets, water, police, fire department, parks, and libraries. Addison delivers those things well.

City Manager Ron Whitehead says, "Those of us in municipal government try to demystify what customer service means. It's really not that hard. Citizens want to know that the sewers work, the streets are paved, and the police and fire departments show up when they are needed. *Results Rule!* is absolutely the way they think. They don't really care what you did for them yesterday. Every day we have to prove ourselves again."

That explains the fundamentals, but what makes the community distinctive?

The first things most people notice when they drive into the town are the attention to detail and aesthetics. The elected officials and municipal employees made these a priority during a time of rapid growth in the 1980s, and they are firmly entrenched in the organization's culture. Addison is not required to alternate plantings in its median strips three times per year. It chooses to because it wants to be seen as the best.

While many communities pick up brush and landscape trimmings once a month, Addison dispatches someone to pick them up within one day and usually on the same day as the call to the municipal department is made. On more than one occasion, residents have called for pickup before completing the bagging of their trimmings and had the crew arrive while they were still working. Additionally, a truck patrols each neighborhood on Mondays to automatically haul away tree limbs and shrubs cut over the weekend.

Speaking of patrols. The police department walks the perimeter of Addison homes while its citizens are on vacation. Most communities do a good job at sanding major thoroughfares when snow and ice hit. Addison also sands the alleys and side streets to make it easier for citizens to navigate. Addison firefighters will come to your home to change the batteries in your smoke detector once a year. And, to top it all off, when was the last time you heard of a police officer being cited for courteous service while writing a traffic citation?

If you are getting the picture that Addison is unique, you are correct. If you are assuming that it is an upper-class enclave of gated neighborhoods, you are dead wrong. The town has a wide range of incomes and housing.

Here Is Why It Happens

Even City Manager Ron Whitehead cannot deny that Addison has benefited from its location and several strategic decisions made 20-plus years ago. Approximately 80 percent of Addison's land is devoted to commercial use in contrast to the 25 to 30 percent in most North American communities. Just over 14,500 people make their home in Addison, even though the daytime population swells to over 100,000 with the people who come to work, dine, and play there every day. Its tax rate is one of the lowest in its geographic area.

Employees and elected officials from a number of surrounding communities have told me that Addison is distinctive because of its cash flow. They are missing the point. Many cities have larger overall budgets than Addison, and it takes revenue to staff city workers to accommodate the influx of the over 100,000 people that work and travel to Addison each day regardless of how many actually live there. Addison is unique because it pursues the best options over the easiest ones. That is in the DNA of the citizens and the staff they have elected or selected.

Ron sees it this way, "Most government groups focus on what they can't do. They indoctrinate employees into why rules must be followed and basically teach them to say 'No' to citizens. We start with a different assumption. We tell every employee from day one to look for ways to say 'Yes' within the boundaries of what is legal and ethical."

Does the culture of your organization promote choosing the best over the easiest? Do you do the hard work of defining what your best is in the minds of your customers? Does everyone see the value in delivering both fundamentals and distinction?

❏ Doesn't Everyone Want ❏ to Pursue the Best?

During a session with the senior leadership team for a 3,500-plus-employee organization, the discussion turned to assumptions we should make about the people on the team. I dutifully recorded all the usual responses on the flip chart—we are competent; we need to stay focused on the goal; most of us do not really want to be here (okay, I assumed that one from their body language).

I asked if we should assume that all employees want to be a hero and develop a culture that delivers meaningful results.

The response floored me.

"Should we or do we?"

Conventional wisdom assumes everyone would want to be a part of and work for a hero organization. That is, unfortunately, not the case. Some people and organizations barely strive to be mediocre. You know the examples:

- Customer services representatives who don't understand the meaning of customer or service
- Fast food which is neither fast . . . nor food
- Manufactured items where a more accurate name for the warranty is the date after which your product will fall apart in a week

Here's the news. If you don't believe everyone wants to be a hero, either you or members of your team are in the wrong place.

Doug Van Arsdale, CEO of CreditSolutions.com, put it this way, "I always assume success. I always see us in the future."

Doug's philosophy has served him well. Credit Solutions grew from 6 employees to over 250 employees in less than 18 months. The company is on track to double in size within another 12 months. And, we're not talking funny-money growth or dot-com style growth without revenues. Doug's philosophy is it has to work small before it will work large. For him, it is a matter of choosing the best and then executing to deliver on those expectations.

❏ More than Money ❏

For *Results Rule!* organizations, the pursuit to be the best extends beyond making money.

The restaurant Mirror chose to be hip, imaginative, and to always deliver great food. Sewell Automotive chose service. First Texas Bancorp chose relationships. Doug Van Arsdale nailed it when he said, "The best rise to the top in every field, and then the money flows."

My volunteer career with the American Heart Association lasted for over 20 years, including a stint as chairman of the board for one of its largest affiliates. The American Heart Association has proven itself to be one of the premier organizations in any arena—profit, not-for-profit, or government.

As missions go, the American Heart Association has a great one: to reduce disability and death from cardiovascular diseases and stroke. It is clear, to the point, and not exclusively focused on fund raising. Yet, they raise a boatload of money every year—over $650 million in 2004.

It would be easy to assume their financial success is connected to their product. Cardiovascular disease is, after all, the leading cause of death in the United States. Roman Bowser, executive vice president of the organization's Western States Affiliate, told me, "It is the passion for the mission that drives the culture. The passion of the volunteers and staff about the mission leads to the success in fund raising. We are always thinking about how many resources we can put in hospitals, how much we can direct to research, and what we can do to help the community."

But a great product is no guarantee of lasting success. Remember the Sony Betamax?

The American Heart Association pursues the best over the easiest in every area of its operations. Its mission is formally reviewed to ensure relevance every three years. The organization has never had to retract a position on scientific research in its history. Not once since its inception in 1924. Their fund-raising expenses in 2004 were 14.4 percent of their overall revenue compared to the 35 percent that the Better Business Bureau suggests in its Standards of Accountability guidelines. Its recruitment, employee development, and top grading process ensures the organization is consistently identifying, developing, and rewarding their best talent.

Here's a news flash—the easiest choice your organization will make is to focus exclusively on the bottom line. We have, after all, been led to believe that business exists for the sole purpose of making money.

Gary Nelon, chairman of First Texas Bancorp with over $700 million in assets, expressed it this way: "Everyone knows we're in this to make money. But our shareholders also want to help our communities. We support community causes and programs, and everyone knows nothing can happen there unless we make money."

❏ Let's Talk about People ❏

Carrie Ardelean, the COO at CreditSolutions.com, told me, "Hiring is the key to the whole thing. It's understanding the skills fit and the culture fit."

Henry Givray says he has to be relentless and unwavering about finding people who fit the SmithBucklin culture. And Gary Nelon told me one reason First Texas Bancorp is successful today is the philosophy of its founder, Grogan Lord, about hiring good people.

Nelon said, "Grogan Lord always wanted to rely on good people to run his business. He just defined good differently. He looked for people who are trustworthy and loyal. We don't have to worry about work ethic."

McKinsey & Company coined the phrase "the war for talent" in 1997. Their assertion is that the caliber of an organization's talent determines its success in the global marketplace. Attracting and retaining talent is one of the most important priorities for every organization.

❏ Talent Does Not Always Win ❏

Here's a fact: At the elite levels of competition, whether it is in sports, the arts, or in business, sheer talent often loses to a *Results Rule!* culture of teamwork, dedication, and commitment. Having the most talented people does not always ensure success.

The men's basketball competition at the 2004 Summer Olympics is a great example. The U.S. team entered the games with an impressive arsenal of talent. And, they were beaten by teams emphasizing the ability to capitalize on the strengths of the team rather than relying on individual talent.

Results Rule! organizations go a step farther in their people decisions. They understand that cultural fit is just as, if not more, important than the individuals' skills. Like everything else we've addressed in this chapter it comes down to choosing and pursuing the best over the easiest.

❏ Get the Sack ❏

You have to love a company with the motto, "Life is uncertain. Eat dessert first." But that's how Amy's Ice Cream based in Austin, Texas, sees the world. A trip to Amy's is like improvisational theater with a side of really good ice cream. Of course, there are very few foods that cannot be improved by adding 14 percent butter fat.

Gourmet ice cream is a "me too" business. There are a number of great products from which to choose in the markets in which Amy's competes. The uniqueness is the experience created by the right people in the right place. It begins with the employment application.

What does an employment application look like where you work? You are probably picturing a form with lots of blanks to fill in and boxes to check. At Amy's, it is a large white paper bag—which no doubt saves them money since they can also use the bags for carryout orders.

Amy's wants creative people with a sense of humor, and what you do with the bag is the first test. You don't get hired if your bag looks like a corporate resume to go. But your chances look good when your bag has been fashioned into a skeleton sitting in a swing for Halloween.

There are many organizations where an individual with the creativity and sense of humor necessary to be hired at Amy's would not be a good fit. You don't want to hire someone at a nuclear power plant based on the abilities to fashion their employment application into a skeleton.

But that's the point. It would be easy for Amy's to take any applicant who looks reasonably qualified based on a standard job application. But doing so would not be the best for them.

❏ The Lilly Test ❏

Carrie Ardelean from CreditSolutions.com believes the cultural fit is even more important when hiring into leadership positions. Remember, this company grew from 6 employees to over 250 in 18 months, and, anticipates reaching 1,000 employees in two more years. They are all about growth.

Like many organizations, Credit Solutions uses a test to determine applicant fit and asks specific questions to ensure the applicant wants to help build a business. Ardelean's secret weapon, however, is Lilly.

The Lilly test was developed accidentally when Ardelean and Van Arsdale stopped for coffee in the lobby of their building. As luck would have it, they struck up a conversation with the shop's proprietor, Lilly.

It turns out Lilly has a knack for observing and analyzing people. She described an individual and asked if he had applied for a job with the company. After they acknowledged simply that the individual had applied, Lilly proceeded to tell Ardelean and Van Arsdale why the person would not be a great fit with Credit Solutions' informal culture. Lilly recognized the mismatch during the brief interaction while the applicant was ordering a cup of coffee.

The easy choice is to assume the answers and behavior we receive in the interview are an accurate representation of the applicant's performance on the job. The best choice is to look for other—even nontraditional—sources to determine fit.

Today, the Credit Solutions leadership team routinely checks with Lilly to see if an applicant or vendor has been in the coffee shop. Passing the Lilly Test has become one of the ways they determine fit.

❏　**The Ultimate Choice**　❏

Pursuit of being the best doesn't always make things easier. Sometimes it requires you to walk away from immediate opportunities for the sake of long-term success.

Henry Givray told me that his team at SmithBucklin is intensely proud of what they do. They believe that

growth is a fundamental element of success in every organization. They also believe in building long-term partner relationships with their client organizations based on
common expectations, trust, strong communication, col-
laborative planning, joint evaluations, and mutual respect. In fact, they only want to work with associations
that feel the same way.

Who can blame them? Working with clients who
want the same things you want and believe the same
things you believe is always easier and more fun.

Then there are the realities of overhead, payroll, the
need for new equipment, and all the other stuff that
every business and leader has to consider at some point.
SmithBucklin has over 600 employees in multiple cities.
There had to be times when the financial demand of the
company kept Henry awake at night.

Henry told me there are four questions they ask when
they are presenting a proposal to a new prospect:

1. Is there a talented and committed group of volunteer
   leaders? An association without a supply of great volunteers is doomed to failure.
2. Is the industry growing or at least stable? No stability
   equals no opportunity to succeed.
3. Do we believe we can make a difference in this association? Can we help them achieve their goals?
4. Do they share common values? Do they believe in
   the same things we believe in?

Henry admitted that the answers to the first three questions can be rationalized. But the answer to question four trumps everything.

Wait a minute. You are telling me clients have to embrace your culture and choices to be selected as a client?

Only if you really want to pursue the best over the easiest.

This isn't a holier-than-thou, we're-cool-and-you-aren't decision for SmithBucklin. It is based on an important realization: Sharing common values with a client releases boundless human potential resulting in long-term success for the client organization and SmithBucklin. It is a simple, yet powerful, truth that Henry follows in every client relationship.

❏ I Admit It ❏

There have been a few clients I didn't really like and worked with only because we were having a slow month. Tell the truth. Haven't you done the same? I asked a friend if his company would walk away from a situation where taking the business would mean doing what is easy rather than what is best. The response was, "Why? Because in the end we're all marketplace whores?"

Results Rule! organizations are unwilling to sacrifice what is best for what is easy. It is a matter of principle and profits.

66

❑   Disastrous Choices   ❑

Even marketplace heroes make mistakes. Here are a couple of examples showing what happens when you don't apply the discipline of choosing the best over the easiest in every situation:

• *Even legends make mistakes.* Harley-Davidson is more than a marketplace hero. They are a legend. When your customers permanently attach your logo to their body, you are doing a lot of things right. Yet even the best companies can make a mistake. Take Harley-Davidson cologne for example.

This idea was wrong on a number of levels. Think of the image. Do you want to smell like the stereotypical Harley rider? And if so, why buy the cologne? Why not just ride a motorcycle in leather on a hot summer day and save the money?

More important, putting the Harley-Davidson logo on cologne potentially alienates your core customers for the sake of easy sales. I suspect that is the reason why the company no longer offers cologne in its product mix.

Matt Haig, author of *Brand Failures,* noted: "Line extension, megabranding, variable pricing and a host of other sophisticated marketing techniques are being used to milk brands rather than build them. While milking may bring in easy money in the short term, in the long term it wears down the brand until it no longer stands for anything."[3]

A single bad choice does not sentence you to terminal has-been status. When missteps occur, learn from Harley-Davidson. Correct the situation as quickly as possible and run—don't walk—back to basing decisions on what is best rather than what is easy.

• *You can oversell a great choice.* I learned a hard lesson from a well-intentioned plan some years ago. The organization with which I was working decided to throw a big party as the kickoff to their "culture change" initiative. They bused their 600+ employees to an off-site location, hired a rock band, provided food and drinks, and featured the CEO in a rousing speech about how this initiative marked a new day in their history. They even dropped confetti at the end of the event.

You can see where this story is headed.

This group thought they were pursuing what was best. There was no way their initiative could ever live up to the hype created by this event, and they doomed themselves to less-than-spectacular results.

The lesson here is simple—pursuing the best over the easiest requires the discipline to ask the third and fourth questions when making important decisions rather than assuming the first idea is the best overall.

❏ What Choice Will You Make? ❏

Your organization operates in a world where other products and services are basically the same as yours. A customer's decision to do business with you or your competitor often comes down to the smallest of differences. A culture where everyone consistently pursues the best over the easiest pays huge dividends in setting you apart. It is the most important decision you will make. What will you decide?

RESULTS RULES

- The most important decision you will ever make is to choose the best over the easiest. Doing that changes everything.
- The difference between *Results Rule!* organizations and others comes down to two things: *Results Rule!* organizations are passionate to their core about what they believe and want to achieve; and they use their passion to drive every part of their business.
- Choosing the best is not about a statement to hang on the wall. It is about the discipline to hold every action and decision to a higher standard.
- Fundamentals are the minimum. Distinctive is the difference.
- If you don't believe everyone wants to be a hero, either you or members of your team are in the wrong place.
- Values and assumptions drive behavior. Behavior becomes habit. Habits drive a culture focused on results.
- Choosing the best people requires much more than recognizing talent. You cannot overestimate the importance of cultural fit.

Chapter 4

Leverage the Power of Partnerships

Our cause must be intrusted to, and conducted by its own undoubted friends—whose hands are free, whose hearts are in the work—who do care for the result.[1]

—Abraham Lincoln

❏ Give Me a ❏
Reason to Help You

A study conducted by Harte-Hanks revealed that over 70 percent of Americans see no clear benefit from being loyal to any company. In other words, your customers see no particular reason to help you succeed.

In fact, your customers only think of you in two situations: They need something immediately or you give them a compelling reason to do so. They are constantly asking, "Why you? Why now? What makes you relevant?"

Results Rule! organizations, on the other hand, transform transactions into relationships that grow into partnerships. They give customers what they want and more.

71

❏ Give'em What They ❏
Came For and Enjoy It

The difference between a marketplace hero and a wannabe often comes down to the willingness and capacity to deliver the goods under less than ideal conditions. Ask the 250 or so people who showed up to watch Peter Noone (the artist formerly known as Herman) and the Hermits perform on a rainy night in May 2005.

Peter is still bringing his brand of 1960s pop music to audiences around the world, and on this particular night he was scheduled to perform at an outdoor festival. About 6:45 P.M., he and the band were probably anticipating a night off. It had been raining since 10:00 A.M., and the chance of a break in the downpour appeared remote. By 8:00 P.M. the weather had cleared and the show was on.

You don't go to a Peter Noone concert expecting songs from Led Zeppelin, Outkast, or Destiny's Child. You want songs by Herman's Hermits.

From "Mrs. Brown, You've Got a Lovely Daughter" to "Something Tells Me I'm Into Something Good" to "It's a Kind of Hush," Peter and the band performed as if their professional lives depended on it. And, they actually appeared to enjoy it. Noone and the Hermits sang, played, and joked with the audience with an energy level you would expect for an audience of 25,000 rather than 250.

They call Peter's fans Noonatics, and judging from his web site (http://www.peternoone.com) they are enthusiastic in their support. On this night, they stood in

72

the rain, sang along, applauded as loud as they could, and purchased all of Peter's T-shirts, CDs, and other stuff.

So here's the question: Are your customers standing in the rain to cheer for you?

What It Means to Build a Partnership

Peter Noone has appeared in some of the largest venues in the world during a career that spans four decades. He has sold millions of records . . . admittedly not many recently, but he's still a recognizable star. There were 250 people, and it was raining. If you were in that situation, is there a chance you would be disappointed? Would you be tempted to cut a few corners? Could you justify giving less than your best and blame it on the situation?

And yet, Noone went out of his way to make the experience special for those in attendance. Scott McKain, writing in his book *All Business Is Show Business*, puts it this way, "Your customers and employees are going to have an emotional experience because of their contact with your organization, whether you like it or not. Your responsibility—and challenge—is to provide them with the kind of emotional connection that will inspire loyalty."

I spoke briefly with Noone after the concert. We discussed another band I had seen a few weeks before. I noted that he did a great show under terrible circumstances while the other band was mediocre at best in an ideal environment. His response says it all, "Some bands out there haven't learned that it is not about them."

No one has performed the exact list of songs hundreds of times. I suspect he becomes bored delivering the same thing over and over again. But, he knows it is not about him. It's about what your customer wants. That is the secret to building customer loyalty and partnerships.

❏ The Friend of ❏
Randy Pennington Card

Dave Churzminski runs the Cantina Laredo in Scottsdale, Arizona. If you find yourself in the Phoenix area and have a taste for gourmet Mexican food, stop in. Ask for Dave, the kitchen manager Justin, or any other manager on duty and tell them you know about the Friend of Randy Pennington card. You will receive either a free tableside guacamole or a piece of chocolate cake with your meal.

I've given away hundreds of cards and told thousands more about them in my presentations for one simple reason—Cantina Laredo successfully transformed me from a customer into a partner. The relationship began because of great fundamentals and evolved because of the connection established when committed employees interact with customers.

Part of the Family

I met Dave when he was the general manager at the Cantina Laredo near my home. My wife and I started dining there because of the food. We continue to dine there over

40 times per year because of the relationship we've developed with the owners, managers, and employees.

The folks at Cantina Laredo make me feel like I'm part of the family. We even have our names engraved on a plaque on the bar. The staff tells me about their children and grandchildren. They even bring me gifts from their vacations.

I could tell you great stories about Cuco the bartender, the three Miguels, Hector, Arturo, Fabian, Justin, and, of course, Dave. But the best example of creating a partnership with your customer is Fernando.

Fernando the Waiter

Fernando puts in our drink order as soon as he sees us walk in the door. Within two minutes of being seated, the drinks are there as well. You could write this off as great customer service provided to a *very* regular customer, but even then, it would be impressive.

Fernando has taken the typical customer relationship to a new level, however. He brought me a T-shirt during a trip home to the state of Jalisco, Mexico. I reciprocated the gesture by giving him a T-shirt upon returning from a speaking engagement in Japan. In perhaps the ultimate example of being treated like a family member, I once told Fernando that I would not be in to dine one particular week due to my travel schedule. He asked if I was planning to bring him a shirt.

I don't just dine at Cantina Laredo, I dine with Fernando, and apparently a lot of others do as well. Over 75 percent of Fernando's tables in a given week are from repeat or referral customers who—like me—request to sit in his section.

Would your business be better if 75 percent of your customers decided that they wanted to give you money every week? Would it be better if your customers asked if they could put on a promotion to send customers to you?

The answer, assuming the customers are the ones with whom you want a partnership, is absolutely.

It Rubs Off

The Cantina Laredo leadership has placed Fernando on the training team for opening new restaurants. The reason is simple—his leadership rubs off on people.

Jose Luis Magana, head of the Cantina Laredo concept for CRO, Inc., told me, "People on the staff see Fernando's results and raise their performance to try to match his. They know he is building repeat and referral business. They see him winning the sales contests. It raises the bar for everyone."

As we noted in Chapter 3, hiring the right people helps, but it doesn't guarantee that your staff will go out of their way to develop partnerships with your customers. Fernando, and his many talented coworkers, choose to leverage the power of partnerships because the Cantina Laredo managers—Dave, Arturo, and others—choose to do the same with them.

There are two types of employees—those who work for your organization and those who are your organization. To build an enduring company, every individual is responsible for being a Fernando. Likewise if you direct the work of others, your job is developing and mentoring the Fernandos on your team.

❏   Employees Don't Care Either   ❏

A survey conducted by the Society of Human Resource Management in 2004 indicated that 75 percent of the nation's employees are looking for new jobs. The Gallup organization estimates more than 22 million U.S. workers are actively disengaged at an annual cost of $250 billion to $300 billion in lost productivity.[2]

The authors of *Loyalty Myths* note that customer loyalty does not necessarily depend on employee loyalty.[3] I agree with that to a point. The customer purchasing an automobile, computer, or even a tax return may be satisfied and even loyal though the employee providing the product or service is not particularly satisfied with the company. Customer loyalty may be tied to price, convenience, or some other factor. The acknowledgment of this possibility does not diminish the power of committed, loyal employees in delivering results that make you a hero in your marketplace.

You can mandate compliance. Commitment, however, is volunteered. The Fernandos of the world stand out because they are so rare. They energize everyone with whom they come in contact. And, they make a positive impact on your ability to build partnerships with your customers. In a service business, they can make the difference between choosing you and choosing a competitor with a similar offering. In a manufacturing operation, a partnership environment with employees can yield the efficiency and effectiveness that allows you to stand out on quality without sacrificing costs.

Unfortunately, disengaged, disenchanted employees make a difference as well.

❑ A Partnership Gone Bad ❑

My first flights during the week immediately following the 9/11 attacks were anxious ones. But, this was not solely based on the realization that an airplane makes an excellent guided missile.

I was standing in line along with the other five passengers boarding my return flight from Minneapolis when I overheard the ticket agent helping the guy next to me say, "Sir, I'm sorry about our poor service today. We have other things on our mind."

Let's review the situation. The total number of people in the entire airport would not fill a Boeing 737. There were three ticket agents at this counter to serve five people. We waited patiently for about five minutes watching the agents in deep conversation and assuming the topic was related to our safety. And the response is, "We have other things on our mind?"

Do you think the company really wanted an employee to use those words in a situation where their customers were already uncomfortable about flying?

An Explanation and an Excuse

The person behind the ticket counter in Minneapolis had learned a day earlier that his company's response in the face of a national crisis was to lay off thousands of people. This wasn't weeks or months after the attacks. It was a matter of days.

There is no excuse for the service we received. On the other hand, I definitely understand the explanation.

Southwest Airlines had a different response. They immediately announced that there would be no employee layoffs. Southwest employees responded by volunteering to do things like cut the grass at the corporate headquarters so the company could save money.

When was the last time your employees volunteered to do something to help you succeed?

The airlines immediately announcing layoffs blamed the layoffs on their lack of profitability and high overhead. And they were correct. They just failed to mention the decades of ignoring partnerships with employees and customers that contributed to their dire economic position.

A unique link exists between building partnerships with employees and loyalty with customers. A culture that makes customers feel important is impossible without a culture that makes employees feel important.

Principles for Building Partnerships

Exceptional leaders in the organizations with which I have consulted and spoken all use different techniques for building relationships. Some rely on the power of recognition. Others emphasize access to senior leaders. In the end, however, their strategies to engage the heart and inspire the mind of others fall into the following categories:

- See and act on a greater vision for people than they see for themselves.
- Provide opportunities for meaningful participation.
- Earn and maintain trust.
- Pay attention to the relationship every day.
- Fight for the right to have great people committed to the cause.

It's More than Compensation

About this time someone is thinking—relationships? You don't know my employees. All they want is money.

And for some, that's true. Money can be extremely important. So let's get this out of the way: If you are not offering a fair compensation package based on the prevailing market, your chance of building a successful partnership with staff and ultimately customers is severely diminished. That said, you cannot rely totally on the compensation package to build partnerships with staff. There are examples of highly paid people delivering miserable results in every industry.

Here's a test: Imagine your ideal job of all time. Do you have the picture in your head? Would you do that job for 1 percent less than you are making today? How about 5 percent? 10 percent? 20 percent? 50 percent?

Almost everyone says absolutely at 1 percent and most people drop out somewhere around 20 percent. But if you said 1 percent or 20 percent, the implication is the same. There is something about that job that makes you willing to do it for less money than you are making today.

So what is it for you? And most important, what would make a job so appealing to others that they would be willing to do it for 1 percent less than they are making today? Answer that question, and you will create an environment where people want to help you succeed.

❏   An Encounter at the Pool   ❏

I met Eva at the Hilton Waikoloa Village in Hawaii. I kissed her, rubbed her stomach, and played with her underwater during our morning at the pool. It was an amazing experience . . . and not what you think. Eva is a 400-pound Atlantic Bottlenose dolphin and part of the Dolphin Qwest program.

It is an accepted fact that dolphins in the wild do not allow humans to kiss them, play with them, or do stunts on command as Eva did that morning. So why did Eva make a customer ecstatic and the owners of Dolphin Qwest look like heroes?

The easy answer is fish—the preferred currency for dolphins. Eva and the other dolphins are on the ultimate pay for performance plan. They give an amazing performance, and they receive fish. But there is more than simple behavior modification at work here.

I spoke with Dawn, one of the Dolphin Qwest trainers, after the encounter and asked her a few questions. I wondered if the trainers had favorites among the dolphins. She admitted that was true.

I also asked her if the dolphins had favorites among the trainers. Dawn's immediate response was, "I've never had that conversation with any of the dolphins."

And after a few seconds of reflection she said, "I hope not. And, I hope they don't know we have favorites."

Dawn told me that the trainers work on two things every day—the performance the customers see and the relationship that fuels trust between dolphin and trainer. She said the time devoted to each is about equal, and everyone recognizes the benefits of focusing on both.

It Works That Way with Humans, Too

Picture a teacher, mentor, or coach who meant a great deal to you. Did that person expect more of you or less of you? Did you do more or less to meet those expectations? Was your commitment based on the person's position or the strength of the relationship?

Here's the news—in a world where the financial benefits of doing business with you are basically equal, the strength of your relationship is the critical element in leveraging the power of partnerships. It doesn't matter if you are dealing with customers, colleagues, or employees. You will never build a culture that blows the competition away without creating relationships that grow into long-term partnerships. Like Dawn's relationship with Eva, it is something that must be addressed every day.

❏ What Do You See? ❏

Randy Gage is a leading expert in direct selling and network marketing. He has personally built a successful network marketing business and helped others do the same. I asked Randy what successful multilevel marketing leaders do to engage people. Here is what he told me:

> The best ones see a bigger vision for their people than they (the people) have for themselves. The leader conveys that vision and nurtures them to grow into it. Most people respond quite favorably, as very seldom do people tell them they are capable of greater things.
>
> This is really a strong engagement, because instead of the new person looking at their sponsor to "save" them, they are working to reward the trust their sponsor has in them. A very powerful relationship develops.

Gage's lessons from the direct-selling industry have an implication for every organization in every industry.

Partnerships have the opportunity to develop when we make a conscious decision to see more in others than they see in themselves. But seeing the potential in others is not enough. It must be communicated and nurtured until it becomes a self-sustaining reality.

Carrie Ardelean's experience working with volunteers in a not-for-profit agency influenced the way she looks at employees. The COO of CreditSolutions.com said, "We are grateful our employees chose us. They volunteered to come here."

Gary Nelon told me that First Texas Bancorp is "blessed to have long-term employees." The message of genuine appreciation is seen by all in the catered breakfasts they have to celebrate tenure and the company's willingness to invest in people.

Gary is quick to note, "Tenure doesn't mean you get to slack off. We reward performance." At the same time, it is evident there is a sense of partnership within the organization.

What do you see when you look at the associates and colleagues you rely on to deliver results that matter to your customers? Do you see a greater vision for their potential? Do you view them as volunteers? And most important, what are you doing each day to act on that vision?

❏ Little Things Mean a Lot ❏

Mary Kay Ash was one of the all-time best at making the results-relationships link and leveraging the power of partnerships. I had the honor of interviewing her during research for my first book, and I'll never forget one of the lessons she taught me: Little things mean a lot.

Most people associate Mary Kay Cosmetics with big things—big pink Cadillacs, big diamond tiaras, and big fur coats. Mary Kay's message to me was big things lose their luster without the little things to prove you are sincere.

Here's an example. During our conversation, Mary Kay asked me, "Have you ever worked for a company that passes out turkeys at Thanksgiving?"

I said, "As a matter of fact, I have."

Mary Kay then asked, "When did you receive the turkey?" And I responded, on the day before Thanksgiving.

Mary Kay went on to ask, "How did the turkey come?"

"Frozen."

"Randy," she asked, "how long does it take to thaw a turkey?"

I have to admit I was stumped.

Mary Kay went on, "It takes one to two days to correctly thaw a turkey. Which means if you don't receive it until Wednesday, someone—and we all know that means the wife—stays up all night thawing it. And then she finally gets a couple of hours of sleep before she's up making breakfast for the children and completing the thawing of the turkey. She then cooks the Thanksgiving meal and serves it in the late afternoon or early evening. And then she cleans up after the meal and finally sits down sometime in the evening to enjoy the holiday."

Mary Kay said, "It's a little thing, but we give our turkeys out on Monday . . . prethawed."

There are two important lessons from Mary Kay's example. First, if you bring home a frozen turkey on the day before Thanksgiving, consider taking the family out for dinner. And second, you can't forget the little things in creating a sense of partnership with others.

❏ The Key Element Is ❏ to Show You Care

There are things you do to recognize specific performance, and there are those you do to simply show you care. It is an important distinction. Recognition of specific performance is an excellent tool for focusing the organization's energy and efforts. The things you do to show you care are the ones that build partnerships.

Mary Kay handed out turkeys to everyone, not just the star performers. And in doing so, the company showed a sense of caring. The event marketing firm One Smooth Stone schedules four half-day Fridays during the summer. Its Mission to Meaning program matches the time and money staff members give to nonprofits. Credit-Solutions.com brings in lunch one day each week for everyone on the staff. Sewell Lexus serves lunch to every employee who works on Saturday.

When Hurricane Katrina ravaged New Orleans and the coast of Louisiana, Wal-Mart provided substantial financial and on-the-ground support for its associates and others affected. Carl Sewell offered every employee in his New Orleans' Lexus dealership assistance in relocating and a job at one of his other operations.

Efforts and actions undertaken out of a sense of caring pay enormous dividends. Linda Arnold, a sales and leasing consultant for Sewell, told me, "I owe this company a lot. They stood behind me during my mother's illness. I have a huge sense of loyalty and desire to help them succeed."

❏ The SGS Tool Journey ❏

Tom Haag's goal at SGS Tool is to create a partnership with customers that goes beyond competing on price. He is quick to recognize that anyone with $350,000 can purchase the same equipment he uses and offer the same products. The company's difference has to be the associates running the machines and representing the brand in the marketplace.

SGS Tool, founded in 1951, became successful under the prevailing business philosophy of the time—a traditional command and control line of authority and execution. The company wasn't a bad place to work by any means. It was simply, like many companies, a place where doing what you are told and not questioning authority are standard operating procedure.

SGS realized in the 1980s that it must abandon a management philosophy based on fear and the belief that employees must be controlled to deliver results in a changing marketplace. The desire was to create an environment that gives the people who do the work equal measures of authority and responsibility.

This decision sounds like a no-brainer today. What company doesn't say employees are our most important resource? On the other hand, there is a huge difference between what is said and what is delivered.

SGS Tool experienced the consequences of the chasm between intent and action early in its efforts as well. Most organizations—even those like SGS Tool with a supportive management team and committed associates—underestimate the challenge in changing the way things have been done for decades. One former company executive stepped aside after realizing he could change on the outside (his language in meetings and support for the company's emerging philosophy) but not on the inside (his true beliefs and assumptions). His comfort in leading from a position of intimidation was too strong and, to his credit, he had the integrity to say so.

After a great deal of trial and error, SGS Tool settled on an approach that reinforces four principles:

1. *Identity:* Understanding the business and how each person fits in
2. *Participation:* Having the opportunity to work together to accomplish meaningful business goals

3. *Equity:* Enjoying a fair and honest return for the effort expended
4. *Competence:* Knowing that every person is capable of doing what needs to be done to help the enterprise succeed

The approach is commonly known as the Scanlon Plan, but the title is misleading. It is really a dynamic process based on the teachings and research of two people: Joe Scanlon, one of the pioneering advocates for labor-management partnerships from the 1940s until his death in 1956, and Dr. Carl Frost, a pioneer in the theory and practice of participatory management and founder of the Scanlon Leadership Network. The purpose of the Frost/Scanlon principles is to transform the culture from an "us versus them" philosophy to one of partnerships committed to delivering results for all stakeholders. In the case of SGS Tool, it involved a choice to invest in equipment, commit to ongoing training and education, create opportunities for meaningful participation, and provide a sense of ownership through gain sharing.

Tom says the most important change the company made was to realize that participation without meaning is useless. SGS Tool associates participate in interviews for open positions and weigh in on disciplinary actions. The company's gain-sharing process ties organizational results to individual results.

Like many other organizations, SGS associates attend required education and training annually (50 hours of it). It is not training for the sake of training, however. Classes focus on *Kaizen* (a Japanese word meaning gradual, unending improvement) and lean manufacturing techniques, cross training, and business literacy. SGS wants to provide every individual with the opportunity to take responsibility for the success of the company and themselves.

Compare this to what passes for participation in most organizations. Managers talk a great game in the employee communication meetings and even begin the effort in earnest. Before long, a series of minor (and occasionally major) discrepancies between expectation and reality emerge. A decision is made for the sake of expedience. An arbitrary action is taken for convenience. And before long, partnerships and participation have deteriorated into a running joke or worse.

The SGS leadership team and associates don't sugarcoat the importance of being consistent, driving the need for personal responsibility at every level, and delivering results. SGS Tool saw a 20 percent growth in its gross margins from 2001 to 2005.

But somehow that doesn't tell the entire story. The strategic decisions and tactical activities SGS Tool undertook have been attempted by multitudes of organizations with limited results.

When you speak with Tom Haag about the company's transformation, he quickly points out that "none of these things would have happened without the support of a great management team and hundreds of ambitious associates."

The core of the SGS Tool story is a sense of partnership. What you see in the company is a shared belief in and commitment to mutual respect, trust, honest communication, and credibility.

❏ The Importance of Trust ❏

According to the Watson Wyatt WorkUSA® 2002[4] study, companies with high-trust levels outperform companies with low-trust levels by 186 percent. The total return to shareholders is almost three times higher at high-trust companies.

Trust is the lubricant allowing relationships to grow into partnerships. Its absence has a measurable impact on performance, morale, open communication, and the ability to retain top people. A company where there is no trust between employees, results in everyone looking out for themselves. Without trust, your colleagues, associates, and customers will not stand in the rain to help you succeed.

Do I have your attention?

Here's a quick way to determine if you have a current or potential trust problem where you work. Walk around the office and notice how many people have Dilbert comic strips on the wall, calendars on their desk, screen savers, or coffee mugs.[5] If the number exceeds 50 percent, you may have a problem.

This is not a slam against Scott Adams' cartoon. I'm simply recognizing that its popularity is probably in direct proportion to the cynicism and lack of trust in the organization. Judging from his incredible success, it is safe to say trust is a bigger problem than most of us will admit.

❏ The Causes of Mistrust ❏

We studied the causes of workplace mistrust in 2004[6] and found some interesting results. Cheating, cooking the books, and unethical behavior were not the top at the top of the list. I was surprised considering the ethical scandals making the news in 2002 and 2003.

It turns out that people are more concerned about day-to-day behaviors affecting them personally than they are about accounting scandals and corporate fraud. The top five behaviors causing employees to mistrust their managers and organization are:

1. Lack of follow-through on commitments made
2. Openness of communication
3. Amount and availability of communication
4. Incompetent or poor decision making
5. Incompetent job performance

Dishonesty does not show up until number six on the list.[7]

Is This You?

Reading study results is a little like seeing the monthly unemployment reports. They are mildly interesting and easy to ignore if you have a job. The story comes alive, however, when you see the actual comments from survey respondents. Here are some of my favorite responses. Do they describe the place where you work?

- If the job market were better, 80 percent of my coworkers would already be working someplace else—we have lost faith.
- You walk on eggshells most of the time and God forbid you had a creative idea, because you would be shot down.
- I talk with others, they worry, we worry together, and time gets wasted.
- When managers huddle up and stop communicating and start using closed doors is usually a signal to start updating my resume.
- Among them, no one person is highly intelligent.
- To put it bluntly, there is seldom an up side to having a conversation with him.
- I think they confuse meetings with work.

❑ What Trust Means ❑ for Your Business

Gary Vlk, a principle at One Smooth Stone, told me, "What differentiates us is how we get clients from beginning to end with our projects. They feel respected, trusted, and appreciated. It transfers from the office to the client site to the event site."

Peggy DePaoli, a director in the Business Process Outsource division of EDS, says that trust plays an important role in the company's growth strategy. She said, "We are constantly reminding people to swim in your own lane and trust your brethren."

It makes perfect sense. Time is wasted, and paralyzing levels of bureaucracy increase when people cannot or are not trusted to do the work they are hired to do. In one of the most vivid examples, one client discovered a process requiring over 40 signatures to post a vacant position and hire a new person. Five of the required signatures were from the same person at different steps of the process.

Most important, a high-trust organization frees your staff to utilize their talent and commitment to make your organization a legend with your customers.

❏ Broken Umbrellas ❏

Two men drive through the residential neighborhoods of Addison, Texas, every Monday. They are called "The Brush Guys." Their job is to pick up brush and landscape trimmings left from any yard maintenance and cleaning that took place over the weekend. I mentioned Addison's unique philosophy about brush removal in a previous chapter, but here is the rest of the story.

It turns out people throw away a lot more than brush, including quite a few umbrellas. The Brush Guys, without any knowledge or direction from their managers, collected and repaired the umbrellas. After a few months, they found themselves with a collection. So one rainy day they took them to the bus stop and passed them out to people who needed them.

City Manager Ron Whitehead told me, "We didn't tell them to do that. I'm not sure we would have even thought of it. But, they did. We simply communicated that we are in the business of serving people and it is okay if our staff does something out of the ordinary. Then we try to trust them to do it."

❏ Are You Willing ❏ to Fight for It?

Brad Zulke, a principle at One Smooth Stone, made a statement that summarizes everything we've been talking about in this chapter. He said, "We realize we have to fight every day, every week, every month to attract, retain, and engage key people."

That's it. That is what *Results Rule!* organizations do. It is reflected in the vision they have for people and the constant attention to the relationship. It is evident in the way they provide meaningful participation. It shows through in the little things done out of recognition and gratitude that they chose you as a leader with whom they can partner. It is trusting people to do what you have hired them to do and earning their trust by honoring commitments and communicating openly.

And here's the deal—when you fight to earn those partnerships people do amazing things. They become customers who stand in the rain to cheer for you.

Pretty cool, huh?

RESULTS RULES

- Your customers think of you in two situations: they need something immediately or you give them a compelling reason to do so. They are constantly asking, "Why you? Why now? What makes you relevant?"
- *Results Rule!* organizations transform transactions into relationships that grow into partnerships. They give customers what they want and more.
- If you want to build partnerships, you must remember, it is not about you. It is about the customer, and it doesn't matter if you are talking about internal or external customers.
- There are two types of employees—those who work for the organization and those who are the organization.
- If you are a leader, your job is to create a staff of Fernandos. Begin by being a Fernando.
- Compensation is an important tool for building a partnership with your team, but it isn't the only tool. You have to build the relationship.
- The best leaders see a bigger vision about what is possible for their people than the people see for themselves.
- Little things mean a lot.

- Participation that is not meaningful is useless.
- Trust is the lubricant that allows relationships to grow.
- A high-trust organization frees your staff to utilize their talent and commitment to make your organization a legend with your customers.
- You must fight to earn and maintain your position as a partner every day.

Chapter 5

Focus the Energy

The qualities I observe in successful athletes are common among people who enjoy success in business. Both love the battle, the journey, the challenge. Both of them consider the final outcome a by-product.[1]

—John Wooden

❏ A Model to Focus the Energy ❏

I doubt the Roman philosopher Seneca intended to write a blueprint for building successful organizations in A.D. 58. Nevertheless, his words from *On the Happy Life* are a useful tool for thinking about how to focus the energy in an organization.

First, therefore, we must seek what it is that we are aiming at; then we must look about for the road by which we can reach it most quickly, and on the journey itself, if only we are on the right path, we shall discover how much of the distance we overcome each day, and how much nearer we are to the goal toward which we are urged by a natural desire. But so long as we wander aimlessly, having no guide, and following only the noise and discordant cries of those who call us in different directions, life will be consumed in making mistakes. . . . Let us decide, therefore, on the goal and upon the way.

The process is simple: Choose the goal based on your core purpose and principles; determine the correct path to reach it; and focus your energy every day on executing the steps necessary to realize success. Consistent execution is the challenge.

❏ The Walton Way ❏

Wal-Mart has grown from a single store in Rogers, Arkansas, to more than 6,000 facilities worldwide and a position at the top of the *Fortune 500*. Regardless of your personal beliefs about their role in the demise of small-town America or American jobs, you have to acknowledge they are very good at what they do. Even its detractors acknowledge the company's processes, systems, and focus on driving down costs are impressive.

So let's put the political stuff aside for a few moments and return to the core principles driving Wal-Mart's growth. Coleman Peterson told me, "Sam Walton was a truly unusual guy. He had great basic values and incredible vision. He was also a tremendous risk taker. There are lots of people with great values and many who have vision. What made Sam Walton unique was his ability to turn vision into action."

Statistics on small-business start-ups and failures show Peterson's assessment is correct. Consider all the

businesses started each year. What are the chances one—
a retailer no less—will become the largest company in
terms of revenue and employment in the world? Let's
look at the numbers.

The U.S. Small Business Administration (SBA) reported there were 572,900 employer firms created in
2003 and 554,800 employer firm terminations the same
year. There is an old adage that 90 percent of new businesses fail within one year. These statistics do not mean
the adage is true. Statistics from the SBA also show that
40 percent of businesses created are still open after six
years. That equates to 60 percent being out of business
within six years and only a 4 in 10 chance a small business will grow into a large company.

Wal-Mart's growth is even more amazing when you
consider its core competency isn't technology or oil or
even manufacturing. The company simply sells mer-
chandise . . . and they do it better than anyone. Walton
was the embodiment of Thomas Edison's statement,
"Vision without execution is hallucination."

Sam Walton operated his business on three core
values:

1. Respect for the individual;
2. Service to the customer; and
3. Commitment to excellence.

As values go, there is nothing particularly unusual about
them. What is unique is the company's consistent ability
to focus its energy on living those values.

Wal-Mart's transportation and distribution system are excellent examples of taking a concept—service to the customer—and focusing the energy to deliver on the promise.

Former CEO David Glass is widely credited with driving Wal-Mart's distribution system. Its cutting edge technology allows the company to know how a specific product is selling at a specific time in a specific store. Every sale is recorded and generates an order to a distribution center that replenishes the stock on the shelf within a day.

There is nothing magic about this technology. Many retailers do something similar. Wal-Mart simply does it better. It goes back to Sam Walton's belief that business is a competitive endeavor in which you have to keep the customer satisfied. Wal-Mart knows decreasing distribution costs is one way it can deliver the competitive results the customer wants and the financial results the company needs.

❏ Turning Vision into Action ❏

So here's a question for you: How do you focus the energy in your organization?

Many organizations dream up initiatives, put up posters, and hold meetings. Some even give people coffee mugs, T-shirts, wallet cards, and other stuff. These are all nice, but they don't cut it if the goal is lasting change.

Results Rule! isn't an item to put on a staff meeting agenda. The goal is to anchor it in the hearts and minds of everyone in the organization. That doesn't happen by relying on slogans and initiatives. People need to see that results are important.

❏   If You Believe It, Say It   ❏

Consistently and convincingly conveying the *Results Rule!* message to everyone on the team is easier when your organization is the size of the restaurant Mirror or the event marketing firm, One Smooth Stone. The challenge is almost unfathomable if you are the size of Wal-Mart.

Focusing the energy begins with communicating your organization's core purpose and principles. The vehicle of choice for most organizations to communicate its purpose and principles is mission, vision, and/or values statements. But as we saw in Chapter 3, a formal statement is not required to get the message across.

Joe Calloway, a partner at Mirror, said, "A formal mission statement just didn't seem to fit our goal of wrapping a fabulous core product with an experience that compels customer loyalty."

How you communicate your purpose and principles is less important than the commitment and discipline to communicate them. One Smooth Stone, with 18 staff members, describes its desired culture and values in three words: Smart, Fast, and Kind. It is the extension of everything they do both internally and externally. Smith-Bucklin, with over 600 employees in three cities, clearly articulates its purpose, chosen values, and pledge in print and on the web. Wal-Mart, with 1.6 million employees, boils its message down into three basic beliefs.

Regardless of how you choose to describe your core purpose and principles, it is important that they fulfill the following criteria:

• *Clear and understandable*: The core purpose and principles are not about marketing messages and buzz words. The words you choose must clearly state what you stand for, and by default, against. Henry Givray put it this way, "The words must be vivid and come alive. Everyone has to understand what they mean. More important, their meaning must become a vital part of everything we do."

• *An extension of who you are and what you believe*: Anyone who knows or works with the team at One Smooth Stone will confirm that "Smart, Fast, and Kind" is an accurate description of who they are and what they believe both individually and collectively. Their commitment to the principles is demonstrated in their work with clients, relationships with employees, and commitment to community.

For SGS Tool, the goal is customer satisfaction, through commitment to continuous improvement of quality products and services. When you talk with Tom Haag you know immediately that he is more interested in performance than philosophy. Yet, he understands the way people approach their job contributes to the manner in which the company's tools do their jobs.

• *Inspiring—about more than money and profitability*: Wal-Mart's core principles say nothing about making money, and they generated over $285 billion in sales in 2005. General Electric's action-oriented values are stated in four words: Imagine, Solve, Build, and Lead. There is nothing about profitability or revenue, and yet General Electric is consistently one of the most profitable companies in the world.

The cynics will suggest that no organization can simply come out and say it exists solely to make the largest possible return for the owners. It is not politically correct. The backlash from critics would be too strong.

And to some extent, the cynics are correct.

Gary Nelon, chairman of First Texas Bancorp, told me, "Everyone knows we are in this to make money. But our mission is to provide a valuable service to and help the community. We support community programs and causes, and none of those things can happen unless we make money."

Cynics point to perceived gaps between word and deed as proof that the words were developed merely for show and not as a tool to focus performance. For every Sony, General Electric, and Toyota that effectively utilizes its purpose and principles to deliver consistent results, there is a corresponding example of an organization that doesn't.

To be clear, simply articulating your core purpose and principles is not enough to focus your organization's energy, regardless of its size. It is merely the first step. But without it, you will never turn vision into reality.

Connecting
❏ Purpose and Goals ❏

It is difficult to find anything written about individual or organizational success over the past 20 years that does not include something about goal setting. Over one million results appear when you plug the term *goal setting* in an Internet search engine.

The problem in most organizations isn't the ability to set goals. It is making the goals meaningful and relevant.

A client once telephoned to ask if I knew of any good university-based leadership education programs. I immediately rattled off several. My client said, "Thank you," and would have hung up had I not stopped him.

It turns out that his boss had assigned him a goal of investigating education programs. The three-minute telephone call allowed him to check off one more box on his annual performance review.

Somehow, I don't believe that is what Seneca had in mind when he said, "Let us decide, therefore, on the goal and upon the way."

SGS Tool utilizes a process called Associated Integrated Management to link the entire organization together vertically, horizontally, and developmentally from strategic plan to employee goals. It is based on the *Hoshin Kanri* concept utilized by leading manufacturing organizations throughout the world. *Hoshin Kanri* is a Japanese term meaning management and control of the organization's strategic direction (compass). It works this way:

- Top management sets the overall vision, annual strategic objectives, and measures of success based on critical business needs and an honest assessment of current realities.
- Each level of the company moving vertically and horizontally develops goals and ensures alignment with strategic objectives.
- Work processes are adjusted to achieve the targets.
- Every associate receives information on how the company is performing, how the division is performing, and how each team is performing versus the company's objectives.
- Processes are evaluated and refined to ensure results are achieved.

The goal of this process is to encourage accountability, responsibility, and expectation in everyone. And while it is most effective when used across the enterprise, the concepts can be applied to divisions, departments, and teams.

If this sounds overly mechanistic, remember the purpose is to develop a set of consistent, understandable, and attainable actions to translate the core purpose and principles into action. Studies have shown a high correlation between understanding expectations and your contribution to the organization's success and job satisfaction. Sirota Survey Intelligence found 83 percent of employees considered "knowing what's expected of them" as something they liked about their job.[2]

❏ Creating Discipline ❏

Peggy DePaoli, a director in EDS's Business Process Outsourcing operation, believes, "Metrics bring discipline. Disciplined minds lead to disciplined actions, and that leads to results."

If you think Peggy is being harsh, you are wrong. EDS lives in an environment where an immediate and effective response to clients and the market mean the difference between success and failure. As Peggy says, "The marketplace brings a hungry culture. We have to stay focused on what works for our customers."

The discipline DePaoli describes is not unlike that implemented with competitive teams in sports, the arts, and even the military. Imposed discipline, when combined with a sense of purpose, becomes self-discipline, and self-discipline allows individuals and groups to focus on and deliver results that matter.

❏ If It's Important, ❏ Measure It

Doug Van Arsdale, founder and CEO of CreditSolutions.com, recognizes that it was easier to tell how well things were going at his company when there were only six people working there. The group would get together over lunch or after work, and often he was sitting right next to people while the job was being done. With over 250 employees and growing today, Doug relies on numbers more than ever. Not only does he look at the numbers every day, every employee on the staff sees their results each day as well.

The principle is deceptively simple: Results occur when you inspect what you expect. And while every *Results Rule!* organization with which I have worked measures and evaluates performance, processes, and progress toward desired goals, they do not do it the same way.

One Smooth Stone conducts client surveys both during and at the completion of projects to allow them to provide feedback. Brad Zulke, the company's COO, stays on top of the numbers while President Kevin Olsen looks at the financial results only occasionally. For the firm's principles, it is a matter of allowing everyone to focus on the areas where they can have the biggest impact.

SmithBucklin provides multiple evaluation checkpoints throughout the year with client leaders. The company uses both formal and informal vehicles to capture information, and many of the questions relate specifically to the "soft" issues of relationships and trust. Henry Givray has discovered that the answers to the soft questions are often the most important. He told me, "When you share common values with client leaders and have built a foundation of trust, small issues become non-issues and big issues become opportunities for mutual problem solving and learning."

There are also multiple evaluation checkpoints, formal and informal, throughout the year for SmithBucklin staff. Becoming a top performer at SmithBucklin requires tangible contributions to the mission *and* living the company's values.

The Town of Addison measures numerous factors surrounding results and processes, but Ron Whitehead quickly adds, "We are not obsessive about it. We measure outcomes more than processes, and we're willing to allow the need to take precedent over the process. We focus on the end result. Does it match the vision?"

SGS Tool takes a more structured approach focusing on results and process. Sales information is updated every 15 minutes and is available on computers in every break room. Results on departmental goals and performance are measured monthly. Tom Haag told me, "It took two to three years of tweaking the measures, but now it is a living document that helps us stay focused."

The common factor among all of these examples is a commitment to measuring what is important to drive performance and the culture.

❏ Three Important Questions ❏

Peggy DePaoli told me there was a time when EDS measured virtually everything. With 120,000 employees worldwide, it is easy to see how you could end up with a great deal of data and very little valuable information. "Now," she says, "we only look at the most important things."

Identifying those most important things is one of the most critical steps you can take to focus the energy. It is easy to measure everything and know nothing. So this is probably a good time for this reminder: Fundamentals are the minimum and distinctive is the difference.

Here are three questions our clients have found helpful in determining their most important performance measures:

- What performance must we deliver and results must we achieve to make us valuable to our customers and profitable in the marketplace?
- What behaviors must we demonstrate to live our values?
- What must we learn today in order to be better tomorrow?

❏ Process This! ❏

An organization's purpose and goals set the direction. Measures focus the energy on outcomes. Processes create habits, and habits drive the culture. You can teach skills and concepts. You can even create momentum (and a few smiles) through inspiration. But investing in skills and inspiration is a waste of money if there are no processes to reinforce your purpose and principles.

The creation and continuous refinement of work processes is a mandatory practice in *Results Rule!* organizations regardless of the industry. People create the systems and at some level the systems influence the people.

Take, for example, the person handling your question at a Sprint PCS Customer Care Center. There is a process (or system if you prefer—the words are used interchangeably at this point) in place to research and respond to your question. The process ensures consistency. It also enables the customer care representative to make decisions consistent with the company's core purpose and principles.

Over time, processes shape performance. And through continued refinement, they allow individuals and teams to become even more effective. The stability created actually provides a sense of freedom. The customer care representative knows the parameters of her authority and the company's goals. With that information in place, she is freed to focus on creating a positive experience.

❏ If It's Important, ❏ Recognize and Reward It

Remember Eva the dolphin from Chapter 4?

There is no doubt that Eva's trainer Dawn developed a strong partnership based on trust with her. At the same time, Eva likes the fish she receives for performing.

Reward and recognition are critical tools for focusing individual and group energy. The challenge is to reinforce the correct behaviors and performance.

The manager (now retired) of a large power plant with which I worked several years ago opened a session with his management team by saying, "As we think about our future, it is important that we realize each part of our operation is connected. We must learn to think and act as a team."

The short pep talk ended, the plant manager left the room, and the participants in my seminar burst into laughter. It was then I found out that while teamwork was the manager's latest flavor of the month, the compensation system in place was designed to reward individual contribution.

It is vital that the reward or recognition system used by an organization actually reward the behaviors that the organization is working toward achieving. Henry Givray and I discussed the reward and recognition model at SmithBucklin. It is a delicate balance because the company's success is based on the success of his clients as well as the company's performance. He said, "80 percent of our bonuses are tied to client goals and the other 20 percent are tied to our overall performance."

❏ Skin in the Game ❏

Skin in the game—providing a sense of ownership—takes many forms in today's organizations. SGS Tool uses a gain-sharing plan to focus its efforts. The program is based on companywide, departmental, and individual performance. Sewell Automotive utilizes a concept called parallel pay to ensure individual performance and rewards are connected to the performance that makes the company successful.

About 11,000 U.S. companies have an Employee Stock Ownership Plan (ESOP) covering an estimated 8.8 million people. This is not a solely American phenomenon. Companies in the United Kingdom, Spain, Italy, Poland, Russia, Ireland, and Slovenia use some form of employee ownership as well. Experiments are under way in Australia, Egypt, Jamaica, Kenya, and South Africa. And, employees in China have been allowed to purchase shares in enterprises owned by the Chinese central government.[3]

It turns out ownership is a powerful motivator. Some form of plan is in place in nearly 80 percent of the companies appearing on *Fortune*'s list of "100 Best Companies to Work For" and in about one-third of *Inc.* magazine's list of the 500 fastest-growing privately held businesses.[4]

SmithBucklin became a 100 percent employee-owned company in 2005. Its decision is a natural extension of its pledge to take care of people so they can take care of clients.

In many ESOP arrangements, the company borrows funds to buy out all or a portion of owners' stake. Employees are granted shares as the company pays back the loan. In the SmithBucklin ESOP, all employees were given the opportunity to actually acquire ownership in the company using their own money to buy company stock. This was accomplished via a one-time election option to move a percentage (0 to 100 percent) of funds in their 401(k) plans or use funds from outside qualified plans (e.g., IRAs) to buy SmithBucklin stock.

The company didn't stop there, however. SmithBucklin crafted its bylaws to reflect a much higher standard for openness, transparency, and trustworthiness than required by law or even put in practice by most organizations. Its bylaws require the following:

- A seven-member board that includes the CEO; three insiders (i.e., employees), and three outsider directors
- The appointment of a lead outside director with certain powers and responsibilities to provide balance with an insider chairman of the board
- An Audit Committee comprised of two outside directors
- A Compensation Committee comprised of the three outside directors plus the CEO with full authority to set compensation for the CEO and other senior executives without the board's approval

Henry Givray told me, "The provision on the Compensation Committee baffled the experts. They couldn't believe that senior management would want to give up control to outsiders. However, since there are four insiders on the board, the insider directors (i.e., senior executives) could in effect set their own compensation. Given our culture, values, and the specific individuals on the board, this would not be a problem today. However, to ensure complete transparency and not even the perception for conflict of interest, we wrote our bylaws to reflect a more stringent provision."

Givray considers the ESOP the highlight of his leadership career. He told me, "I fundamentally believe that it's our people, day in and day out with their hard work, dedication, and many, many contributions that are creating value in SmithBucklin. As such, they are the ones that should have the opportunity to experience the rewards and fulfillment of ownership, not outsiders. For me, it was this principle that drove me above all else to make this transaction a reality. In addition, by being a 100 percent employee-owned company, the control and destiny of the company remains in the hands of our people."

Now for the real question—does it make a difference in results?

Based on anecdotal evidence after several months, Henry and the leadership at SmtithBucklin believe true skin in the game has strongly reinforced both the Smith-Bucklin culture and its commitment to deliver extraordinary value and service. Givray says, "Our people get how critical it is for our company to cultivate, protect, and reinforce the SmithBucklin culture if we are to build an enduring, great company. The ESOP has made this point very tangible and real since success not only means wonderful careers and compensation opportunities, it can also mean wealth creation."

Tom Haag at SGS Tool agrees. Though his company is a second-generation family-owned business and does not have an ESOP, its gain-sharing program (called TEAM for Together Everyone Achieves More) is the culmination of the culture the company has been working to create since 1990. Tom says, "The program has helped associates understand exactly what we are trying to accomplish in their work center and how this helps the overall corporate objectives to be met. It has created a true sense of team to know that their contributions must be coordinated with others in order to be successful."

Implementing a gain-sharing program is an extremely motivating benefit to provide employees, however, you must be sure that your organization is capable of successfully executing such a program. Before you run out and create a program that allows associates to put skin in the game, consider this cautionary note from Haag: "The only thing worse than not having a gain-sharing program, is having a gain-sharing program and taking it away."

❏ It's Amazing What ❏
They Will Do

I had the honor of conducting several management training sessions at Ft. Eustis, Virginia, home of the U.S. Army's Transportation Corps. While visiting on the base, I walked through the museum that houses the various modes of transportation used by the army through the years. Near the front of the museum was a wall displaying the various battle campaign ribbons that have been given to soldiers in recognition of their service. Above this impressive collection was a quote from Napoleon stating, "It is amazing what a man will do for a piece of colored ribbon."

The cynic points to Napoleon's quote as an indictment on how little it takes to buy someone's loyalty.

117

Those who have earned one of those ribbons in combat know that the true value is not in its cost but in the effort it represents.

❏ Not Everyone Gets a Ribbon ❏

Recognition is a valuable tool for building self-esteem and results. Every organization should encourage all who actively participate and strive to improve the operation. But *Results Rule!* cultures do not confuse activity with accomplishment.

The movie *Meet the Fockers* takes a humorous look at everything that can go wrong when prospective in-laws from totally different backgrounds meet for the first time. In one of my favorite scenes, the father of the bride, Jack, is viewing the trophy wall dedicated to his future son-in-law's accomplishments. The father of the bride turns to the father of the groom and says, "I didn't know they made ninth place ribbons."

The father of the groom replies, "Oh, Jack. They got'em all the way up to tenth place."

What do you want to see hanging on the wall when you walk into your physician's office—a certificate that says "Board Certified" or one that says, "Participant"?

There is a place for acts designed to promote camaraderie and loyalty. And there is a time to focus the energy on performance that makes a difference. Be very clear about your goal and do not confuse activity with accomplishment. It sends a powerful message.

❏ Tell the Story ❏

Quick—prove the geometric theorum for a polyhedral triangle. Remember, you learned it in high school.

No luck? How about reciting a favorite story from your youth? Much easier isn't it?

Before the written word, information was passed on orally, often through the use of stories. Stories create pictures and touch emotions that permanently embed meaning in our hearts and minds. *Results Rule!* organizations use stories and legends to drive home key lessons about the culture.

One Smooth Stone asks new staff members to read the documentation of their first 72 hours in business contained in their *About Us* handbook. The company's leaders want new people to understand its roots are very humble, beginning with a staff of three people sitting in folding chairs before a single computer.

Similar to the leaders of One Smooth Stone telling their company's history, Ron Whitehead kicks off every new employee orientation program in Addison by sharing stories about superior service and what it means to work for the Town of Addison. Quarterly Employee Service Award luncheons are viewed not only as an opportunity to celebrate tenure but also to add to the organizations history of stories and legends.

Coleman Peterson, former executive vice president and chief people officer for Wal-Mart, immediately told me a story about Sam Walton when I asked him to talk about what makes the company's culture unique. He went on to explain the influence that hearing about Sam Walton from their leaders and seeing him had on the associates' behavior. The company newspaper, spring and fall meetings, videos, and live broadcasts are all designed to share more than facts and figures. They share the stories that focus the energy and reinforce the culture.

Stories and legends are powerful tools for sharing experiences and conveying meaning. They shape the awareness and behavior of individuals and groups. Telling your organization's stories makes the core purpose and principles come alive and helps employees feel a part of an organization's legacy. We may not remember the facts, but the stories stay with us forever.

❑　The Sewell Way　❑

Sewell Automotive Companies is obsessed with providing a level of service that turns one-time buyers into lifetime customers. Many companies tout their service as the thing that sets them apart. Most of them blow it. Their idea of a customer service initiative is to send people to a training program on how to be nicer.

Like Amy's Ice Cream (mentioned in Chapter 3), Sewell places a great deal of emphasis on hiring the right people. But, Carl Sewell knows that providing excellent service requires more than hiring great people. Here are five things Sewell Automotive does to focus the energy in addition to putting people with good attitudes in place:

1. *Teach people the culture from day one.* New employees are given a copy of Carl Sewell's, *Customers for Life* on their first day of orientation. Sewell is not the only company to use the written word to communicate what is important. It just takes the effort more seriously than most. Linda Arnold, a sales and leasing consultant at Sewell Lexus, shared this story about an early training experience and how it taught her about the company's culture.

> We had been given Carl's book as a reading assignment, and I blew it off. I figured they would tell us everything we needed to know so why should I read it. Right before lunch, the instructor asked us to number a blank sheet of paper from 1 to 10. And, we had a test on the reading assignment. That was bad enough, but then we returned from lunch and the scores were posted alphabetically on the door. There was my name with a "FAILED" beside it. I was so embarrassed, and I aced every exam that followed. Most important, I immediately understood the culture— people are expected to take responsibility for doing the things that make you successful.

Orientation into the Sewell culture extends beyond the classroom. Jaquita Deaton, a service manager at Sewell Lexus, told me, "It takes two to three months for a service writer to completely understand our way of doing business. When you come to work here, you work in the shop assisting the technicians, in parts, in pick up and delivery, in loan cars, everything. The group teaches you the Sewell culture."

2. *A process for everything.* Want to know how to open the service department at a Sewell dealership? There is a step-by-step process with standards for measurement. There are also processes for cashier interaction with customers when they pick up their automobiles and greeting customers on the service drive. From the most mundane to the most complex, if a job involves customer interaction, there is an expectation defining the Sewell Way. Some might balk at the assumed rigidity of so much structure, but the Sewell staff sees it differently. Deaton told me, "The structure actually provides a sense of freedom since you know what to do to succeed. There is always a game plan for success."

Freedom within structure is a lesson understood by great improvisational musicians. There are infinite possibilities for self-expression within the structure provided by the tempo and key. Without them, inspired performances turn into chaos. Processes ensure stability and consistency. As Jaquita noted, "You can tell when someone starts to deviate from our processes because their numbers go down. They are not doing it the Sewell way, and our customers notice it."

3. *Continuously measure and provide feedback.* Linda Arnold's training experience was an indicator of things to follow. Sewell Lexus measures every significant aspect of its performance. Its internal call center follows up on every service call and provides daily feedback to managers. Sales numbers are continuously updated and posted for all to see. The same is true for repair work that must be done a second time. An outside firm shows up unannounced on the service drive to evaluate how well the Sewell customer care processes are being followed. The first 45 minutes of Deaton's day are set aside for reviewing progress toward monthly goals in the service department. Every discussion ends with a plan to adjust processes to meet forecast. Linda Arnold summed up the company's use of measures and feedback, "I know how I'm doing and where I rank, and I don't want to be at the bottom."

4. *Use the best for inspiration.* Sewell Lexus is an innovator not an imitator. That is why it is the number one Lexus dealership for service in the United States. Jaquita said, "We are always looking for ways to differentiate. Most of our competitors are now offering loan cars. We were the first in the Southwest to do it. Others have service and rescue operations and tow trucks. We started that, too. We use companies such as the Four Seasons, Disney, and Ritz Carlton for inspiration, but we are always looking for ways to improve our processes."

5. *Reward performance.* Sewell Automotive utilizes a concept called *parallel pay.* The premise is simple—ensure the interests of the employees and the dealership are aligned when it comes to compensation. Commission is the compensation driver for sales and leasing professionals. For service technicians, it is the number of jobs completed correctly and at a profit. No one gets paid for rework. For managers, compensation is based on the net profitability of the department. For support functions, measures contributing to profitability and service levels are utilized.

Like other *Results Rule!* organizations, Sewell also understands that recognition can be its own reward. A board displaying the certifications voluntarily earned by each service technician hangs in the shop. It is a matter of pride that focuses everyone's energy on being the best.

❏ **Where We Go Wrong** ❏

Why is it that some organizations utilize the tools and techniques described in this chapter to deliver amazing results while others use them to foster mediocrity and alienate others? The answer often centers on two words—passion and soul. The best organizations show it. The others do not.

A core purpose, goals, processes, and measures can be used to create meaning or can become dreaded obstacles that suck the joy out of coming to work. The difference lies in the manner in which they are used. *Results Rule!* organizations know that passion for work and genuine concern for people provide a powerful context for building an enduring organization. They maintain a sense of balance between the structure required for consistent, predictable performance and an unwavering belief in the power of individuals to make a difference.

Kevin Olsen from One Smooth Stone explained the difference between processes and procedures that help and those that hurt: "A lot of business owners try to wring as much out of their people as they can. We see a definite advantage to help our people maintain a sense of balance."

That's what Sewell Automotive did when it provided relocation and jobs for its employees left without work after Hurricane Katrina. That's what Southwest Airlines did when it supplemented the income for the company-employed skycaps that rely on tips until air traffic revived after 9/11.

Read the quote from Seneca at the beginning of this chapter again. The noise and discordant cries to which he referred are those that tell us we can focus the energy without honoring the value of relationships. The individuals and organizations divorcing the two will be consumed in making mistakes that diffuse their energy rather than focus it.

RESULTS RULES

- If you believe it, say it. Articulating your core purpose and principles defines the direction and provides focus. Strategic plans are worthless unless you know where you want to go and the rules by which you want to arrive there.
- Many have great values and vision. What makes you unique is the ability to turn vision into action.
- Metrics bring discipline. Disciplined minds lead to discipline action, and that leads to results.
- Processes provide structure.

- It is amazing what people will do for meaningful recognition.
- Stories and legends share experience and convey meaning.
- Tools to focus the energy have the power to transform when combined with passion and soul.
- *Results Rule!* isn't an item to put on a staff meeting agenda. The goal is to anchor it in the hearts and minds of everyone.

Chapter 6

Show the Courage
of Accountability

To act and to know are one and the same.

—Old Samurai Maxim

I think our number one problem is that nobody wants
to take responsibility for anything—but don't quote
me on that.

—Anonymous Manager

These words, uttered by a frustrated manager during research for my book *On My Honor, I Will*, sum up the disillusionment felt in many organizations and across society in general. It relays the common sentiment that individuals often make excuses when their performance falls short rather than admitting mistakes. Elected officials and government agencies at every level shift blame for failure to deliver promised results. Managers allow employee performance that does not meet expectations to continue without consequence. Corporations play fast and loose with accounting standards and principles of responsible governance. The list could go on and on.

The ultimate distinction setting a *Results Rule!* culture apart from all the others is personal and organizational accountability.

❏ We Know the Words ❏

The walls of our organizations are covered with posters describing the characteristics we want to emulate. Speeches are given. Meetings are held. Memos and wallet cards are distributed. Every organization does it . . . even those with no apparent intention of living by them. Enron, for example, put the words *Respect, Integrity, Community,* and *Excellence* on coffee mugs and a huge banner in their corporate headquarters.

Perhaps it would be better to throw the words out rather than display them and then not live up to them. At least people will only think you are stupid rather than dishonest in your intentions.

❏ It's about Leadership ❏

The level of accountability within an organization has a direct correlation to the quality of leadership. You either accept responsibility for your actions and decisions or you don't. You create an environment that allows people to bring their best selves to the job, or you don't.

As we discussed in Chapter 1, good leadership does not require an individual to be in a position of authority. The position merely ensures compliance, and there are times when even that is suspect.

Remember when as a teenager you were caught sneaking out of the house to hang out with your friends? Even after being punished by your parent or some other authority figure, did you quit sneaking out? Or, did you get better at it?

Let's assume for a moment that you are able to use your position in the organization to mandate compliance. Is that really the level of performance for which you want your company, team, or project group to be known? It hardly shouts *Results Rule!* does it?

Compliance can be mandated. Commitment is volunteered. The difference comes down to fundamental issues such as respect, credibility, showing confidence in others, developing the capacity to perform, and trust. If you cannot be trusted to keep your word and deliver on promises, your rhetoric about building partnerships is unlikely to be taken seriously. If you are not known for delivering results, it is safe to assume others will not willingly go above and beyond the status quo to help you succeed. And, if you cannot do those things, the chances of building an organization that delivers consistent results are minimal at best.

❏ We Wanted to See ❏ What You Would Do

Early in my career I was on the senior leadership team that opened a state-operated residential treatment center for children and adolescents. Our residents were between the ages of 10 and 17, and very few wanted to be there. Needless to say, "runners" (residents who tried to run away) were common.

The senior leadership always wore suits in those days, which doesn't make a lot of sense looking back on it. On one particular day, I was standing in front of the administration building with a group of staff and residents when a teenage boy made a break for it. I looked at the staff, and they looked at me. I waited for someone to take off after the youngster, and nothing happened. I decided to give chase in my suit and dress shoes, and an amazing thing happened—others followed.

Our chief nurse stopped by my office a few hours later, shut the door, and said, "You passed."

She went on to tell me, "We were curious what you would do." In their eyes, I was a young guy who should be able to at least make the effort to help. They didn't expect me to catch the runner. They only expected me to be accountable . . . to lead.

Herb Kelleher, chairman, president, and CEO of Southwest Airlines, earned the respect of his staff by periodically loading bags onto airplanes and greeting passengers on flights. Wal-Mart executives spend time in stores every week. Kevin Olsen and Gary Vlk, principles at One Smooth Stone, are intimately involved with client projects and pitch in to do whatever it takes to make a production successful.

People want to see what the leader will do. Once they know you are responsible and committed, most will readily join the chase for results.

❏ Two Levels of Accountability ❏

Accountability for results occurs at two levels: individual and organizational. The two are obviously connected.

For most people, a respected leader (regardless of position) modeling personal responsibility and encouraging others to do the same is all it takes to foster a sense of accountability in a team or group. The influence of positive role models isn't limited to the boss. Athletic teams often talk about the importance of veteran leadership in the locker room. They realize the power of positive leadership and peer pressure.

There is always a small percentage, who will not take personal responsibility for their actions and decisions. For this group, an organizational system of accountability is a must.

Even then, influencing another to take responsibility requires personal courage. Most organizations have some process for providing feedback and encouraging accountability. But, even the best system requires a level of personal accountability to achieve desired change.

❏ **Let's Get Personal** ❏

Professional athletes prepare mentally and physically for an entire week to play a game that lasts a matter of hours. So wouldn't you expect each of them to readily accept responsibility when the game is on the line? After all, that is what they are paid very well to do.

The professional and Olympic athletes with whom I've spoken over the years all say the same thing—you can look in the faces of teammates and competitors when success and failure are on the line and tell who wants to accept responsibility and who doesn't.

Michael Jordan, the legendary professional basketball star and winner of six National Basketball Association championship rings, describes his drive this way, "Whether it was competing with my siblings or trying to get attention from my parents, I wanted to show what I could do, what I was capable of accomplishing. I wanted results, and I was driven to find out the best way to get them."[1]

There's a line from the often-quoted "Unknown" that applies here, "If you really want to do something, you'll find a way; if you don't, you'll find an excuse."

Personal accountability usually comes into question when we don't want to do something out of fear or disinterest. Fear plays a role in situations where failure has a personal impact. That could explain an athlete's reluctance to take responsibility when the game is on the line. It also explains why some managers have difficulty granting greater authority for decisions or confronting performance that doesn't meet expectations.

Disinterest, intentional or inadvertent, is also a factor in adopting and implementing personal accountability. It is not uncommon for managers to move on to the next project or crisis before a new initiative is completed, and leaving employees to execute the previous priority. Those who never wanted to change to begin with are perfectly content dropping the ball. Disinterest is an enabler of the status quo.

Either way, the result is a lack of execution, and that will get you fired. Ram Charan has suggested that 70 percent of the reasons why CEOs fail can be attributed to problems with execution.[2] Mark Murphy, chairman and CEO of Leadership IQ, concurs. He reports that lack of execution, including tolerating low performers and not taking enough action, is much more damaging to your career than strategic blunders.[3]

Wait a minute. Are you saying accountability and execution are more important than strategy?

In the long run, yes. Core purpose and principles rarely change. Strategies, however, must continually evolve to meet marketplace demands. A mediocre strategy well executed usually wins out over a great strategy implemented with mediocrity. In short, great strategies fail without great leaders at every level.

You cannot hope to influence others to follow without proactive commitment and genuine comfort in taking responsibility for your own decisions, actions, promises, and results.

❏ Top-Down or Bottom-Up? ❏

Historically, the responsibility for creating and driving the culture rests primarily with those in positions of power, and to a certain degree that is still the case today. The Southwest Airlines culture is a direct product of its leaders' commitment to people. Wal-Mart's culture continues to reflect Sam Walton's personality. SmithBucklin's Henry Givray believes articulating, aligning, protecting, and nurturing an authentic culture is one of the leader's most important responsibilities.

So does that mean the time you have devoted to this book is wasted unless you are a CEO? Hardly.

Team leaders or managers can also create their own *Results Rule!* culture. The idea that there can only be one corporate culture shared by everyone is a myth. Sure. One corporate culture exists in small companies like One Smooth Stone and the restaurant Mirror. But does anyone really believe that the culture is exactly the same at every Wal-Mart store or even at all of First Texas Bancorp's multiple branches? The culture in the police department in Addison, Texas, is different than the one in the special events department, but both exist very comfortably within the town's overall culture of service and excellence.

How about if you are not in a position of power?

Remember that we are talking about influence. Leaders at all levels influence the content of the discussion, and you don't have to be in a position of power to accomplish that goal.

If you have worked in an organization for any length of time or at the very least watched *The Apprentice,* you know that one person can make a huge difference in the culture of any group—especially if he or she has a negative attitude.

One of the most compelling aspects of the Internet is the ability of anyone to influence the content of conversations. The Drudge Report regularly influences the international media. Employee blogs spread the word about what people in the organization are really thinking. Chat rooms and web sites exist to share opinions—good and bad—from staff members and customers.

So here is my response to the top down or bottom up question. The best way to ensure your culture blows the competition away is to engage leaders at every level to be accountable for action that delivers meaningful results. If you are in a position of power, be accountable for leading. A culture that distinguishes you in the marketplace is at best difficult and probably impossible unless you do.

If you are not, don't underestimate your power to influence others. I'm not saying you have to kiss up to the boss or be the lead singer in the corporate choir. Just realize you don't have to be a *suit* to make a difference.

❑ Pumping Water ❑

In the days following Hurricane Katrina and the flooding of New Orleans, the Army Corps of Engineers predicted it could take three to six months to drain the flooded city. It was accomplished in a matter of weeks.

The heroes of this effort were about 300 New Orleans Sewage and Water Board employees who did the work of 1,000. This group worked nonstop, some wearing clothes given by others, to get the city's system of large screw pumps running and then keep them going until the effort was completed.

Managers and nonmanagers worked side by side to deliver important results. It is likely that the culture of the New Orleans Sewage and Water Board will be forever changed because of their courage and accountability.

❏   Holding Others Accountable   ❏

I have asked the following question to participants in management and leadership development programs for over 20 years, "What is the toughest part of managing people and performance?"

I can't think of the last time the responses didn't include, "holding people accountable and addressing mistakes."

A participant in one session told me that his company did not have a problem with accountability or poor performance because it had fired fewer than five people in a workforce of thousands over the past five years. Another participant quickly replied, "That's the problem. No one ever gets fired for anything."

I'm not suggesting a quota system for terminations. But, my guess is that in most organizations of more than a handful, there are people who are not being held accountable for delivering the results you need to stand out. Those doing a good job know who the noncontributors are, and it would make their lives much easier if those with the ability to do something about it would act.

❑ How Do You ❑
Approach Accountability?

There are a variety of different approaches for holding others accountable. General Electric and other companies use a forced ranking system that requires a specific percentage of staff to be identified as low performers each year.

Forced ranking has supporters and enemies. The few organizations doing it well have developed a process consistent with their culture. They were already very good at ensuring accountability. Forced ranking is simply another tool for them. The large number doing it badly did a lousy job of ensuring accountability in the first place. Forced ranking introduced as a quick fix for years of bad leadership is a disaster waiting to happen for your culture.

And that's the key—finding a process that works for your culture and situation.

One Smooth Stone, for instance, assigns a mentor to every member of the team. Every person has a performance plan containing goals about financial performance, skills, attitudes, and culture to guide them. Any problems are addressed individually. Team members hold each other accountable. Team members also ensure accountability at SGS Tool with associates recommending disciplinary action for those not meeting their goals.

First Texas Bancorp and the Town of Addison utilize more traditional performance appraisal processes.

Many of the organizations with which we've worked adopted a POSITIVE PERFORMANCE® management process based on the following core beliefs:

- Individuals deserve to be treated with integrity and respect.
- Most people want to do a good job and will do so if given the opportunity and ability.
- The leader's job is to create the environment for employees to succeed as individuals and as a group.
- Everyone is responsible for performing in a manner that helps the organization achieve results and build strong relationships.
- Treating individuals responsibly means that we earn the right to expect them to act responsibly.

Organizations as diverse as the Alabama Power Company, Sprint PCS, and Texas A&M University have experienced measurable improvements in numbers of disciplinary actions and retention in addition to performance and productivity improvements once they decided accountability is a positive thing.

138

❑ The Fear of Confrontation ❑

So if we adopt a new process, our accountability problems are solved right?

Wrong.

The last 350 words were devoted to accountability processes because most of you are using displeasure with the your organization's approach as the excuse for not holding people accountable.

The truth is that the percentage of noncontributors, those not fulfilling their performance requirements, is small—probably 2 percent to 5 percent. The U.S. federal government found that 3.7 percent of their own employees are poor performers so let's assume your numbers are no worse than theirs.[4]

The real reason we don't do a good job addressing performance problems has very little to do with not having the proper processes or having large numbers of people who should be gone from your organization. It is the discomfort (and fear) of confronting others that enables poor performance. Most of us are not able to constructively confront others at work. We don't do it well in other parts of our life either.

The Toothpaste Story

See if this sounds familiar: On the first morning of our marriage, I noticed my wife squeezes toothpaste from the middle of the tube. I, on the other hand, follow instructions that say (this is the part where the anal retentive people speak along with me), "For best results, squeeze from the bottom and roll up."

You might not think this is a big thing, but the little things often destroy relationships, trust, and accountability. Remember the demise of WorldCom started out as just one little change to some numbers on a ledger.

I thought to myself, "You should say something to her about this." But fear sets in. I could see myself standing in the bedroom. My wife of less than 24 hours is still asleep, and I'm holding a tube of toothpaste screaming, "What is this?"

It wasn't a pretty mental picture so I did what many of you would do. I squeezed up from the bottom, returned it to the holder, and assumed it would be a one-time, single-incident occurrence that would be self-correcting once I modeled the correct performance.

This went on for a couple of months—her from the middle, me from the bottom. During that time, we went to visit her parents. I had been there before, but now I was seeing with new eyes. Her mother and father have separate bathrooms.

I walked into her mother's bathroom and there it was—squeezed from the center. I thought, "I'm on to something."

Later that day, we went to visit her grandmother—her mother's mother. I found an excuse to leave the conversation and peek into her bathroom. And there it was . . . not just squeezed from the center. It was more like mangled from the center, and now I know I'm dealing with a hereditary problem that will only get worse with age.

I finally reached a breaking point. One morning I turned to my wife and said, "Don't you know I hate this?"

My wife looked at me and smiled . . . providing my first clue she had been doing it on purpose.

She said, "Oh, sure, I knew that two months ago."

She was laughing. Me . . . not so much.

I bellowed (at least that's her version), "If you knew it two months ago, why did you keep doing it?"

She responded, "You're the hotshot consultant. You travel all over the world helping people achieve results, communicate more effectively, be accountable, yada, yada, yada. I wanted to see how long it would take before you would mention it to me."

She was laughing more. Me . . . still not so much, and I said, "I'm mentioning it to you now. What are you going to do about it?"

Her response was, "It's a seventy-nine-cent problem. If it means that much to you, I'll buy two tubes."

I am not the only person to ever have this experience. The problem wasn't with my wife. It was my unwillingness to be accountable for confronting something that bothered me.

In fact, if I had gone to my wife at the first appropriate opportunity and simply said, "Honey this might not seem like a big deal, but it is important to me." One of two things would have happened:

1. She would have said, "No big deal. It's a seventy-nine-cent problem."
2. If you actually knew my wife, you would know that her more likely response would have been, "Seems like a personal problem, you'll have to get over it."

Either way the problem is solved.

This is an opportune time to ask that you not suggest I purchase—or worse send me—one of those metal keys to attach to the bottom of the tube. Trust me. It will not be well received.

The important question is, "How often do seventy-nine-cent problems become huge issues in your organization?" You know the ones I'm talking about, those that grow so large and looming you have to call a special meeting or get people several levels above you in the organization involved to solve.

The courage to confront is how you make the culture stick.

❏ **You Don't Fit** ❏

Carrie Ardelean, COO at CreditSolutions.com, was extremely excited the day she told me about the new department manager joining the team. He was from an organization with a great reputation, and his skill set was impeccable. It became a different story in a matter of weeks.

I asked Carrie how the new manager was doing, and she said, "He's gone. We let him go after three weeks."

Theft? Inappropriate behavior with a colleague? Coming to work impaired in some way? Those were the things that came to mind. Why else would you terminate a promising manager within a short time period?

Carrie answered, "He didn't fit our culture."

She went on to tell me about the small signs appearing almost immediately. There was little effort to meet the members of his department and lots of time spent behind closed doors. The final confirmation was a demeaning comment made to a staff member two levels below him in a meeting. The tone told Carrie and CEO Doug Van Arsdale that this wasn't going to be a fit. In their mind, there was no choice but to let him go before the culture was affected.

Carrie is no different than you and me. She doesn't wake up in the morning thinking, "I get to fire someone today." She does, however, share a characteristic with leaders who consistently deliver results. She has the courage to confront.

❏ Brutal Decisions Don't Mean Brutal Conversations ❏

Henry Givray from SmithBucklin agrees that confronting people is never pleasant, but he goes on to say, "You have to be relentless and unwavering about looking

143

at contributions people make to the mission and behaviors consistent with our values."

Do not take an unyielding focus on results as justification to be a jerk with people. Taking that approach will cost you talent, destroy partnerships, and at best, ensure compliance when you need commitment. Tough decisions about performance and contribution do not have to mean brutal conversations.

The ability to confront others without being confrontational is so important I want to spend a moment on specifics for holding a conversation. Here are six ideas you can use in a partnership approach to confronting performance:

1. *Prepare first.* Create an outline of points you want to cover. Keep the focus on the performance and results not the person. Describe the expected and actual performance using specifics. Make a list of the good business reasons why the issue must be addressed and the potential consequences if performance doesn't change. Before the meeting, walk through the conversation in your mind. Anticipate issues that could come up. You are more likely to keep your cool if you are prepared.

2. *Bring the issue to the individual's attention in a specific, behavioral, and nonthreatening manner.* The first few seconds of the conversation will set the tone so choose your words wisely. Describe what you expected and compare it to the actual performance or behavior you observed. Ask the individual to describe what happened from her/his perspective. Listen and respond appropriately. This is a partnership and the purpose is to solve a problem.

3. *Gain agreement about the nature of the problem and build ownership for results without sacrificing the relationship.* It is surprising how many people fail to ask anyone to agree to do anything differently or discuss a plan to make things better. So go ahead and ask, "I would like your agreement to resolve this in the future. Can I count on you?"

Most people will agree, and when they do say, "I appreciate your agreement. What do you plan to do to live up to those good intentions?" You can offer to help where appropriate, but remember to keep the responsibility with the individual.

4. *Look forward positively.* There is very little motivating about a conversation that consistently beats someone up for what happened in the past. And if you are convinced the individual has no future with the organization, why don't you just terminate him? This is the time to remind the individual of the hopes and aspirations you have for him or her in the future.

5. *Write it down.* Adjust your level of documentation to the seriousness of the issue. If it is something minor, make a simple note to remember the conversation. If it is serious, write a memo summarizing the conversation, agreements, potential consequences for continued performance, and your positive expectation for the future. Most people create documentation before the conversation, and that's a mistake. How would you feel if someone handed you a piece of paper then said, "Read it and sign it. Now let's have a meaningful discussion?" If your company has a policy about these things, follow it.

6. *Follow-up to reinforce resolution, provide support, and continue to build the relationship.* If an issue is important enough to have a conversation, it is important enough to follow up. This closes the loop on the conversation and lets the individual know the solution is equally as important as the problem.

Taking this approach to confronting problems makes it easier for everyone involved. As Walter Graham, Compliance Manager—Ethics and Business Practices at the Alabama Power Company noted, "Employees can initiate dialogue with supervisors, knowing that they are willing to talk and to help work out problems, rather than acting as an adversary."

❑ The Actual Cost of ❑
Seventy-Nine-Cent Problems

There is a difficult balance between the need for compliance and the desire for commitment. There is security in knowing the rules are being followed, and a sense of freedom in skilled and committed individuals given the opportunity to deliver amazing results.

Being open to ideas, opinions, and initative from others can be scary for those who believe accountability is primarily about compliance. It has the potential to slow down decisions and even action. That is why some prefer people not to make waves and always follow the rules.

My food service manager at the residential treatment hospital for which I was an administrator viewed the world in this way. I walked into the kitchen one day to find the message "Do the job. Don't ask questions!" painted above the door leading to the serving area.

I was shocked and had the sign immediately removed. The associates on his team seemed to take it in stride. For me, it was the first visible sign of trouble. For them, the sign simply reinforced the message they heard every day.

Fortunately, the cost of this manager's view of accountability only affected morale and our ability to keep good people. That is bad enough, but it could have been much worse.

January 28, 1986, brought the horrific images from the space shuttle *Challenger*'s destruction to our television screens. The explosion taking seven heroes raised questions about competence in the U.S. space program as we wondered how a catastrophe like this could happen.

The visible culprit was an O-ring. The demanding specifications to which parts are built for space travel no doubt made this more than a seventy-nine-cent problem. Yet, compared to the overall price tag to build and maintain a space shuttle and the irreplaceable cost of human life, the price of an O-ring is indeed small.

It turns out there was a second, more dangerous culprit in the explosion of both the *Challenger* and, 17 years later, *Columbia* space shuttles. It was a culture where fear about speaking up regarding safety concerns was pervasive. NASA Administrator Sean O'Keefe spoke of, "a NASA mind-set that says, 'We've got things to do, we've got to get on with this, we don't have time to listen to everybody moan and groan about every issue out there."[5]

❏ **Giving People Control** ❏

Leaders in *Results Rule!* cultures recognize the necessity of compliance, and they embrace the transformation that comes from giving individuals control over their own results. For them, it is not an *either/or* question. Choosing the best over the easiest demands they do both.

Preparing individuals to be in control of their own decisions and results requires the leader to:

- Clearly communicate the core purpose, principles, and expectations.
- Provide the necessary knowledge and skills.
- Define the boundaries for individual action.
- Give the trust and freedom to fail in honest pursuit of the purpose and principles.

Those who have been the parents of teenagers know the simplicity of the words is deceiving. Remember (or imagine) when your teenage son or daughter drove the family automobile for the first time? The parents with whom I've spoken over the years describe the experience as stressful. One person said, "The night my teenage son drove by himself for the first time, I went to bed at 8:30 P.M. and slept like a baby. I woke up every two hours and cried."

❏ Two Types of Mistakes ❏

Everyone makes mistakes. They come in two types: mistakes of the head and mistakes of the heart.

Mistakes of the heart are those when your head knows the right thing to be done and your heart convinces you to do things for the wrong reason. Mistakes of the heart are the decisions and actions violating the core principles. People who make this type of mistake wreak havoc in your organization. If you are in a position of power, get rid of them as quickly as possible. If you are not in a position of power, let them know what they are doing is wrong, give them a chance to make amends, and if they don't, report them.

Mistakes of the head are the honest mistakes made in pursuit of the core purpose and organizational goals and in keeping with your principles. These are learning opportunities. You don't get to make them forever, but you should have the opportunity to correct, grow, and move forward.

Think of the most important lessons you have learned in your life. How many of them came from mistakes?

I can only think of one really important lesson I ever learned from another's mistake. At the age of 16, my

149

brother was caught sneaking out at night and taking my father's pickup truck joyriding with his friends.

I saw what happened to him, and I learned from his mistakes. Of course, I didn't have a younger brother to tell on me.

❏ All You Need to Do ❏
Is Take Responsibility

Carl Sewell of Sewell Automotive told me, "Organizations spent a lot of time on processes a few years ago. And processes are certainly helpful. But, accountability is as important—and may be even more important than—processes."

Imagine the potential cost savings and results generating innovations if everyone simply took responsibility for delivering the results you know are important to blow your competition away.

I know it is difficult. You don't want to look foolish if it doesn't work out as planned. You don't want to deal with a difficult confrontation. Or, you think it is not your job.

We know what can happen if you choose not to be accountable for your own performance and the performance of others. We've seen the results of assuming accountability is only about compliance.

What's the worst that could happen if you were accountable? Mistakes are a part of life, and not taking responsibility is a mistake in itself.

So go ahead. All you need to do is take responsibility.

RESULTS RULES

- The ultimate distinction setting *Results Rule!* organizations apart is personal and organizational accountability.
- Leadership is the art of influencing the actions and outcomes of others to achieve results. It does not require a position of authority. Accountability is ultimately a leadership issue.
- The members of your team know if you are accountable or not when results are on the line. And, those doing a good job appreciate it when those who are not performing are held accountable.
- Fear prevents us from confronting performance that does not meet expectations.
- Tough decisions about performance do not require brutal conversations.
- Seventy-nine-cent problems grow into major issues when left unaddressed.
- Value the importance of compliance and embrace the transformation that comes from helping others be in control of their own results.
- There are two types of mistakes—mistakes of the head and mistakes of the heart. Mistakes of the head are learning opportunities.
- The best way to ensure your culture blows the competition away is to engage leaders at every level to be accountable for delivering meaningful results.

Chapter 7

A Love Affair with Results

I hate losing. I mean, I love winning, but losing is a much more intense feeling. When I lose, I take it very personally.

—Jennie Finch

Past successes are proof that you have been right once. A loyal customer will cut you some slack for an occasional bad day, but a steady stream of disappointments will cost you. The difference between a dynasty and the sporadic winning year comes down to the ability to consistently be better tomorrow than today. Think of it as a love affair with results.

John R. Weeks, assistant professor of organizational behavior at INSEAD, suggests that "journalists, investors, and analysts will praise a company's culture as long as the company performs well and makes money."[1]

As the old song says, "Nobody knows you when you're down and out."[2]

❑ Excellence Revisited ❑

Tom Peters and Bob Waterman Jr. changed the world of business books in 1982 with the publication of *In Search of Excellence*. The book profiled 43 companies identified as excellent. Two years later, *BusinessWeek* magazine ran a cover story questioning the authors' choices noting that several of the companies cited had delivered less than stellar results.

It is true. Several of the companies turned out to be not so excellent after all. Some—such as Wang Labs and Atari—fell quickly. Others—such as Kmart and Delta Airlines—flourished for years before falling. And a few— IBM and Xerox for example—hit hard times and rebounded. Overall, however, Peters' and Waterman's list of excellent companies has done pretty well for itself.

If you had invested $10,000 in the 32 public companies cited as excellent in 1982 and never touched it, you would have amassed $140,050 in 20 years. The same investment into the Dow Jones Industrial companies would have yielded $85,500. In short, the public companies on Peters's and Waterman's list earned an average total return of 14.1 percent annually compared to an 11.3 percent return from the Dow Jones Industrial Average companies and 10.1 percent from the Standard & Poor's companies.[3]

So here's the question we should all want to know: What is the difference between the Intel's, Wal-Mart's, and Marriott's of the world that continue to thrive and those that have slipped into obscurity?

Merrill (Rick) Chapman believes he has the answer for the high-tech firms highlighted in *Excellence*. He suggests that they failed to learn from the past and repeatedly make the same avoidable mistakes.[4]

❑ Are You Learning ❑
from the Past?

An unexpected guest appeared at a project design team meeting in Virginia for the Huntsman Chemical Company. The operations manager from the Woodbury, New Jersey, plant had been included on the meeting announcement list as a courtesy. No one expected him to actually fly in for the meeting.

At the first break, I thanked him for attending. He responded, "That's okay I didn't really have much to do today anyway."

The comment caught me off guard since the plant operated 24 hours a day with a very aggressive production schedule. I laughed and said something like, "I'm sure that's not true."

He explained that he worked about 45 hours per week except in the summer when he took off early on Wednesday afternoons to play golf. Approximately 50 percent to 55 percent of his time was devoted to operational issues, meetings, and the routine running the plant. He devoted 25 percent of his time each week to follow-up, coaching, and team development. The remaining 20 percent to 25 percent of his week was devoted to thinking about and planning for the future. The project on which I was consulting fell into the last category, and he thought it wise to attend.

I asked how long he had maintained that schedule, and he explained that he had been at the plant for several years. The schedule had evolved as his team had improved its ability to learn and perform more effectively. Here is how it worked: The operations manager would drop whatever he was doing to solve a problem the first time it appeared. The time of day or day of the week didn't matter, and he stayed with the problem (working side by side with the staff) until a solution was found and implemented. Since the majority of the problems were process related, the second step was to ensure that updates and education took place throughout the entire organization. Because he wanted to promote an environment that learns from mistakes, the individual identifying the problem often received recognition. He then went on to say, "There is, however, a different conversation if a problem appears a second time."

Admittedly, the pace of change has increased exponentially since this exchange took place. Yet, the principle still has merit. Many organizations continually shoot themselves in the foot by repeating the same mistake again and again. After a while, they think walking with a limp is normal.

A great way to know if you are learning is to place your organization on the following continuum. At the upper end, you are solving 100 problems one time. At the lower end, you are solving one problem 100 times. The closer you are to the upper end, the better job you are doing at learning from past mistakes and the more likely you are to be truly satisfied with the results you are achieving.

❏ Learning from Past ❏ Mistakes Isn't Enough

Focusing on the past—even if it is to learn from mistakes—is no longer enough to give you an edge. Change and leadership expert Dr. Terry Paulson says, "The action is out the front window; that's why your rearview mirror on your car is smaller than the windshield."

The big issues facing your business in the future have to do with globalization, delivery systems, organizational structure, talent development, and the prospect of some dramatic event making your product or service obsolete. Delivering results tomorrow depends on how quickly you can change; how much you can learn; and how much passion you bring to the effort.

❏ You Believed Her? ❏

Prior to our marriage, my wife said, "Randy, I'll never ask you to change."

I thought, "Cool!"

She went on to say, "I do expect that you will continually adapt."

Sort of sums it up, doesn't it?

By this time, everyone should be aware that demands are increasing and change is constant. If this is news for you, there are big problems headed your way. The issue is no longer if everything in your business will change. It is how quickly you can anticipate and adapt.

❏ ## Culture— Accelerator or Anchor? ❏

Everything we've discussed to this point extols the virtues of a strong culture as the ultimate tool to blow the competition away. But there is a dark side. Your organization's culture can also be an anchor that holds it back and prevents it from adapting to a changing future.

Bethlehem Steel stood at number 8 on the *Fortune* 500 list in 1955. By 2002, it had dropped to number 440. The International Steel Group purchased it in 2003. The company's culture of insulated decision making, out-of-date work rules, and slow response to market changes became an anchor to continued viability.[5]

Xerox, one of the companies featured in *In Search of Excellence,* lost touch with customers and failed to move into the digital age. The bureaucratic aspects of its culture overshadowed its rich history of innovation. It allowed seventy-nine-cent problems to grow until the only alternative was drastic action.

My wife's suggestion that I change the way I think about change is good advice for everyone. The secret is to develop an adaptive culture that respects the past while remaining open to future opportunities and challenges. And, the best way to accomplish it is by changing more, rather than less, in pursuit of the core purpose.

❏ Change Change ❏

The CEO of a 3,000 employee organization with which I consulted called his 75 top managers into the conference room and opened the meeting with these words:

> I have been here just over two months, and I have spent much of my time getting to know how things are done. I have come to the conclusion that General Motors in the 1950s was more flexible, fast, and customer focused than we are. Things are going to change.

While the choice of words might be suspect for some of you, it is important that you know this organization needed to be shaken rather than stirred. There are times when you just need to lay it on the line. That no-nonsense approach has been a hallmark of Anne Mulcahy's leadership in turning Xerox around.

Like Mulcahy, this CEO laid out a dramatic vision for the future. He then went on to orchestrate six reorganizations in 18 months.

Why so many? Couldn't they get it right?

The driving force behind the series of reorganizations was the belief that the organization must continuously adjust how it does things to meet the changing demands of the marketplace. There were no mass layoffs associated with any of the reorganizations just a series of sometimes dramatic and sometimes subtle realignments of resources to focus on serving the customer.

The ability to adapt to and anticipate change is a habit, and the only way to develop new habits is to go through a period of discomfort. It is a message shared in the early 1960s by Thomas Watson Jr., then CEO of IBM: "I believe that if an organization is to meet the challenges of a changing world, it must be prepared to change everything about itself except (its) beliefs as it moves through corporate life."[6]

❏ Think Transition, Not Change ❏

Xerox returned to profitability after near bankruptcy due to sound and inspired leadership from Mulcahy and the thousands of employees who committed to saving the company. And while their effort is impressive, is waiting until a crisis emerges the only way to break the anchor of the past ?

We must look no farther than General Electric to know the answer is no. A *Fortune* magazine headline trumpeted, "Another Boss Another Revolution" to describe Jeff Immelt's decision to change the direction established by his predecessor (and legend) Jack Welch. Of course, that is the same thing they said about Welch, and the CEO before him, and the CEO before him.[7]

Life is a continuous state of transition. That is especially true for organizations. Here are five ideas for maintaining the sense of urgency required to deliver results year . . . after year . . . after year:

1. *Generate creative tension.* Crisis produces a sense of urgency. So does opportunity and maintaining the underdog spirit. Dell Computer and Wal-Mart have more than their low-cost strategy in common. Both have maintained a hunger for success by focusing on opportunity rather than always waiting for crisis. Creative tension to achieve more is the natural outcome when a compelling vision is tempered with reality. Dell may be the leader in personal computer sales in the United States, but there are many other markets and product lines where opportunity exists.

2. *Ensure the "important stuff" continues.* EDS is passionate about success and honesty. Peggy DePaoli noted that its senior leadership places a high value on people development, creating tools for employees to succeed, and being honest. What is the important stuff in your organization? Customer service? Producing a product? Maintaining an ethical environment? Whatever it is, make sure it continues. Anne Mulcahy cut over $2 billion out of Xerox's cost structure without touching Research and Development unlike Maytag, which cut new product development in half.[8] You can't deliver results without ensuring the important stuff continues.

3. *Set the stage for the future.* The Town of Addison conducted its first visioning process in 1994. The result was a recommendation for how the community should look, feel, and act in the year 2020. Ten years later, another group looked ahead to the year 2030. Unlike most communities, the Addison strategic visions were not designed as the first step in a bond election to build things. In fact, the Town did not pursue bond funding on a single project until several years after its first vision document was completed. The purpose was to build a compass not draw a map. Ron Whitehead has carried the notion a step farther by asking his staff to develop "innovation statements." Ron says, "Its not just about best practices. We are looking for areas where we can plough new ground."

4. *Respect the past.* Many years ago I played a lot of tennis. My racquet of choice was one of the best you could purchase: a Wilson Stan Smith model. It was made of wood, had a small face, and felt like its weight should be measured in pounds rather than ounces after a match.

I could still compete today while playing with that racquet, but it would be extremely difficult to win if my competitors were playing with the latest equipment made from a space-age composite with a racquet face the size of a trash can lid.

The practices that frustrate you today were someone's innovative solutions of the past. Do not criticize them. Accept them for what they are and realize that, as the saying goes, "Insanity is doing what you've always done and expecting to achieve different results."

5. *Recognize this day will end.* My ophthalmologist ended my last eye exam with these words: "Randy, your arms will be long enough for another couple of years." If you can relate to my situation of changing eyesight as you age, you know that everything comes to an end. Yet,

I am constantly amazed by leaders, organizations, and entire industries that refuse to acknowledge and act on this truth. As Intel CEO Andy Grove says, "Sooner or later, something fundamental in your business world will change."[9]

❏ What Are You Learning? ❏

This quote from Arie De Gues, retired head of planning for Royal Dutch Shell, has been repeated and modified since it appeared in 1988: "We understand that the only competitive advantage the company of the future will have is its managers' ability to learn faster than their competitors."[10]

So why mention it here? First, because it's true. And second, it doesn't go far enough. Learning can only be a competitive advantage if it extends to every individual within the enterprise.

SGS Tool's commitment to 50 hours of education annually per person was mentioned in Chapter 4 as a tool to build partnerships. Like many of the strategies discussed in this book, this one has a dual purpose. Remember, SGS doesn't do education for the sake of education. Everything is focused on improving the individual's ability to succeed.

Sewell Automotive invests 40 hours of education per year in each of its management staff members. Non-managers are provided significant opportunities for training and education based on the demands of the job. Carl Sewell estimates that approximately 75 percent of the focus is on areas related to your job. The other 25 percent is on people skills. Sewell frequently sends associates to the Dale Carnegie course to improve their people skills.

Carl has also been known to engage in learning for the sake of learning. Craig Innes, former vice president of marketing and human resources for Sewell Automotive, shared that he and an associate were sent to a weeklong course on strategic planning. Upon returning, the two colleagues presented Mr. Sewell with a plan to redirect the company's efforts. They were surprised when they learned the reason they were sent to the program had nothing to do with changing the company's planning process. Carl just felt it would be beneficial for them to have the knowledge and experience of attending.

Why does an automotive company send technicians to Dale Carnegie and executives to programs where there is no immediate job application? Carl Sewell understands the value of learning. In fact, he believes that knowledge is one of the most important things a company can do to ensure lasting results. If you are a better person, you will be a better associate.

Albert Einstein once noted, "We cannot solve the problems of today with the same thinking that gave us those problems in the first place."

Being better at your current job is important, but learning to think differently is the key to solving problems that have not yet been encountered.

❏ How Much Do You Care? ❏

What do Brad Anderson (CEO of Best Buy), Tim Duncan (All-Star forward for the 2005 NBA Champion San Antonio Spurs), Mark Cuban (Internet billionaire, founder of HDNet, and owner of the Dallas Mavericks), and Jay Leno (host of NBC's *Tonight Show*) have in common?

When Brad Anderson talks about the competitive edge at Best Buy, he says, "I'm looking for a cultural edge that regenerates, that allows you to always be dissatisfied and always reinventing. In our industry, with the amount of innovation that's going on, I don't think there's any choice."[11]

Tim Duncan commented immediately after winning the 2005 National Basketball Association championships: "We can play a lot better. That sounds horrible as we sit up here as NBA champs."[12]

Jay Leno is known for being perhaps the hardest working person in show business. Despite over 20 years as host of the number one late night television show on U.S. television and 125 to 150 personal appearances each year, he spends most Sunday evenings testing new material at the Hermosa Beach Comedy and Magic Club. Leno says, "This sounds silly, but my attitude is, sooner or later, the other guy is going to have to eat, drink, go to the bathroom, get laid, or take a vacation, and that's when I catch him."[13]

Mark Cuban sums up the similarities: "It's not who you know. It's not how much money you have. It's very simple. It's whether or not you have the edge and the guts to use it."[14]

The edge these leaders share in common is a deep passion for competing, contributing, and yes, winning. It's being dissatisfied with the status quo, always reinventing, and never resting on your laurels. It is caring so much that you work your tail off to deliver better results tomorrow than you did today. Passion for delivering results drives learning and embracing change as a way of life. It's an attitude not a skill.

❏ You Can Influence It ❏

While you can't teach an attitude of caring, you can do a lot to reinforce it. Coleman Peterson told me, "Culture is not a self-fulfilling prophecy."

He went on to explain that building the passion for results and the Wal-Mart culture begins in the orientation process. Protecting the culture is a topic at each Saturday Morning Meeting and the sole subject of the meeting on the first Saturday of every month. The company uses legends and stories to drive the message home. Its spring and fall meetings include a heavy dose of reinforcing the passion for success. Most important, Wal-Mart associates look to their leaders to live the culture. Peterson says: "Our associates hear about Sam Walton from their leaders. Most important, they see Mr. Sam in their behavior."

❑ Are You Willing ❑ to Walk Away?

The most challenging test of an organization's commitment to its culture and its desire for long-term results is the willingness to walk away from immediate business that is not consistent with its core purpose and principles. It may sound crazy so allow me to explain.

The balance sheet at First Texas Bancorp is relatively simple and, by some standards, conservative. CEO Gary Nelon, along with President John Kirkpatrick, has built solid core deposits and a great deal of discipline into the organization.

Gary told me that he periodically receives calls from industry consultants and product vendors to show him how the bank could be making more money. The pitch is the same: You could make more if you leverage more.

Gary and John are always looking for ways to grow their business, but they refuse to deviate from their core philosophy. As Gary says, "We make good money and sleep well at night. Why would we want to change?"

❑ Integrity Matters ❑

There are two types of people and organizations: those who deliver consistent results without sacrificing their integrity and those who don't. One of my clients refers to this as the "squishy stuff."

The subject of integrity is too often limited to questions of personal conduct. For Nelon and other *Results Rule!* leaders, the decision to walk away from a situation that is inconsistent with its long-term purpose and principles is an issue of both organizational integrity and long-term viability. These two factors are completely inseparable. *Results Rule!* leaders care about long-term results so much that they are unwilling to violate their culture and suffer the potential impact of their decision.

Kevin Olsen, a principle at One Smooth Stone, told me, "There have been groups where the work was absolutely in our sweet spot. We just looked at it and said, 'That is just not who we are.'"

In the movie *Cool Runnings*, John Candy starred as Irv Blitzer, a disgraced American Olympian who is convinced to coach the Jamaican bobsled team. In one scene, we learn that Blitzer was disqualified from an Olympic competition for cheating. In the quest for winning at any cost, he created a situation where he would never again achieve the results he cherished.

Blitzer tells the captain of the Jamaican team, "A gold medal is a wonderful thing. But if you are not enough without it, you won't be enough with it."

❏ Is It Culture or Is ❏
It Following the Leader?

Experience tells us that cultures can fade away without leadership attention. Yet, if the culture requires consis-

168

tent attention is it really part of the organization's DNA? Or, are people merely trying to please the boss? If an organization's beliefs, values, and purpose are truly ingrained, shouldn't they survive the presence or absence of one person?

Herb Kelleher has stated that Southwest Airlines will do just fine when the time comes for him to completely walk away.[15]

Yet, my conversations with leaders suggest that maintaining a culture focused on results is not a guarantee. Coleman Peterson said, "A culture will lose its way without leaders paying attention."

The history at EDS reinforces that belief.

For many years, the culture at EDS was widely considered to be an important contributor to its success. Over the years, a series of leadership changes occurred, and both performance and the culture suffered.

Peggy DePaoli noted that things began to change when new senior leadership came on board in 2002. Their focus was on people, culture, relationships, and giving people the tools they need to perform. She believes pride in the brand is back because performance and culture came back.

Paying attention to the culture makes sense for an organization of 1.6 million employees like Wal-Mart, but how much is required at smaller organizations? The principles at One Smooth Stone, with 18 employees, said culture gets more face time now than ever before. Their approach is to add systems as they grow and develop to ensure the culture translates from folklore to a consistent way of life. Brad Zulke said, "We are a long way from being perfect. Our commitment is to continually get better at every aspect of the business—especially the culture."

Gary Vlk, a principle at One Smooth Stone, compares it to the other star of late night television, David Letterman. "When you watch the show, it looks natural and fun. Dave throws things, and it just happens. Yet Letterman is known for meticulous preparation and attention to detail. On the surface, our culture looks casual and fun. Below the surface, there is a strong foundation and constant attention."

Putting the right people in place makes a difference as well. The culture of the American Heart Association has been refined and advanced by CEO Cass Wheeler and his team. However, the leadership of former CEO Dudley Hafner laid the foundation. Roman Bowser told me, "If you look at the people running our large organizations today, many of them worked for Dudley. He always set a high bar, insisted on a sense of urgency, believed in having fun, and thought about getting better."

The legacy of a great leader is more than immediate results. It extends to the capacity they leave behind. Perhaps that is why Herb Kelleher is comfortable with the long-term staying power of Southwest Airlines. A base of talented people, including COO Colleen Barrett and CEO Gary Kelly, is in place and remain committed to the cause of leveraging a compelling culture to deliver results.

How Long Does It Take to Build a Compelling Culture?

That's a question that often comes up in consulting engagements, seminars, and presentations. My answer is a definitive, "It depends."

There are several questions to consider:

• *Are you starting from scratch or changing an existing culture?* Many of the companies mentioned here have made their culture an essential part of their business model from day one. A few others have changed or altered their culture after the company was in existence. Tom Haag says it took two to three years for SGS Tool to begin seeing the payoff from their efforts. Results as well as the culture at EDS started turning around within a few years as well. Experience and research suggest that time frame is normal if there is a legitimate and consistent effort.

• *What is your history and how much time do you have?* The grocery wholesaler mentioned in Chapter 2 never made the change. There was too much history and not enough time to overcome it. Alternatively, SGS Tool had good relationships with employees before it began its efforts.

• *What is your commitment level?* If your heart is not in it, it won't work. The people and organizations discussed as positive role models in this book really do have a love affair with results that is grounded in the strength of their culture. I think Coleman Peterson hit the point: "The question is do you have the staying power to implement and accept the consequences?"

Gary Nelon has a favorite saying: "Fast birds don't fly far."

Building a culture that blows the competition away takes time, energy, and commitment. It is hard work. You can't install it like a piece of computer software and walk away. If examples from great organizations of all sizes in a variety of industries don't convince you of the benefit or you are looking for a quick fix to your problems, you are probably best served by pursuing another strategy.

❏ **Let Go of the Strut** ❏

When I tell people I have tried skydiving, the first question is often, "Why would anyone want to jump out of a perfectly good airplane?"

I tell them it's the fault of my best friend of 25 years. His name is Charlie Brown. I know what you are thinking: parents who would name their child Charlie Brown are just too lazy to tease that kid themselves.

Charlie and I were sitting in our local hangout when he asked: "Have you ever thought about jumping out of an airplane?"

Here's a hint—when your best friend asks this question, there is usually an ulterior motive.

"I've always thought it would be fun," I responded.

Charlie immediately responded, "Good, because we're signed up for a week from Saturday."

And that is how I ended up standing on the wing of an airplane at 3,500 feet.

There are two preferred ways to experience skydiving for the first time. A tandem jump straps you to a master skydiver for a jump from about 10,000 feet. People choose this method because they free-fall for about one minute; and if you freak out, there is someone there to pull the cord for you.

The second way is a static line jump. This is basically the old military style jump where the main chute deploys automatically from a line connected to the airplane.

The static line is from a lower height, but the biggest difference is the sense of personal accountability. There is no one out there but you if for some reason the main chute doesn't open. You have about 14 seconds to cut away the main chute and deploy your reserve or end up as the second story on the evening news.

We chose the static line.

The training for our jump took about six hours. Four hours of it consisted of what to do if the chute doesn't open. There are several opportunities to back out during the day. A couple of people from our class didn't return from lunch. Another person chose not to go up after completing the training.

For those who have never gone skydiving, here's how it works: Five people are crammed into a small plane for the jump—the pilot, the jumpmaster, and the three newbies with a death wish. Once the plane reaches the desired altitude and location over the drop zone, the jumpmaster tells the pilot to cut the engine.

The door swings open and bangs against the wing—whap. The jumpmaster looks at you and says two words which by themselves are not particularly intimidating, but in this context cause a level of anxiety similar to an Enron executive at an IRS audit—GET OUT.

You swing out of the airplane; grab the wing strut with your left hand; place your left foot on a piece of metal approximately the size of a 5 by 7 photo, and grab the strut with your right hand. Your right foot is now dangling free, and the wind is blowing in your face at about 60 miles per hour.

You look in at the jumpmaster, and he's smiling. You . . . not so much.

And then he says two other words which in any other context would be completely unassuming—LET GO.

You let go of the strut, arch back, and experience several seconds of disorientation followed by the ride of a lifetime.

After my first jump, I asked my instructor if anyone ever freezes on the wing strut and has to be helped back into the airplane. Not surprisingly, that happens on occasion.

And it started me thinking. Why would someone go through all the training and put himself or herself in position for an incredible ride only to back out at the last minute?

Ultimately, it comes down to the fear of letting go of their perceived safety, trusting their ability, and being accountable.

Individuals and organizations do their own version of freezing while standing on the wing.

We know that products and services are for the most part commodities delivered in a "me too" environment. We know that a culture where everyone comes to work every day confident in his or her value and excited about the opportunity to succeed is the ultimate competitive edge. And yet, we freeze rather than take the important (and difficult) step.

My guess is that you know where you need to begin and what you need to do to build a culture that blows the competition away. If you need a reminder, here are the six things *Results Rule!* organizations do more of or better than other organizations. They:

1. Tell themselves the truth and value candor and honesty.
2. Pursue the best over the easiest in every situation.
3. Leverage the power of partnerships both internally and externally.
4. Focus the energy to make the main things the main thing.
5. Show the courage of accountability.
6. Learn, grow, and improve every day.

When I asked Gary Nelon what he considers to be the most important thing in building a culture that consistently delivers results he said, "Just do it."

All the good intentions, training, and desire are worthless unless you decide to let go of whatever it is that is keeping you and your organization from the ride of a lifetime.

So here's my challenge to you. Stop standing in the way of your own success.

If you really have a love affair with results, build (or at least contribute to) a culture that will take you there. Take it personally. Go ahead. Let go of the strut. Just do it.

RESULTS RULES

Past success proves you were right once.

- *Results Rule!* organizations strive to solve 100 problems 1 time rather than 1 problems 100 times.
- Culture can be an anchor or an accelerator. Build one that continually anticipates and adapts.
- The problems and challenges of the future will require a different level of thinking.
- Integrity matters. Be willing to walk away from opportunities that are not consistent with your core purpose and principles.
- Building a culture that consistently blows the competition away is hard and ongoing work. It is not a self-fulfilling prophecy.

- *Results Rule!* leaders and organizations have an edge—
  a deep passion for competing, contributing, and yes,
  winning. It's being dissatisfied with the status quo, always reinventing, and never resting on your laurels. It is
  caring so much that you work your tail off to deliver
  better results tomorrow than you did today.
- Identify the things that are holding you back from
  building the culture you want and let them go.

Notes

Chapter 1: It's the Culture, Stupid!

1. John Huey and Geoffrey Colven, "Staying Smart: The Jack and Herb Show," *Fortune* (January 8, 2002).

2. Joe Calloway, *Becoming a Category of One* (Hoboken, NJ: Wiley, 2003).

3. John Huey and Geoffrey Colven, "Staying Smart: The Jack and Herb Show," *Fortune* (January 8, 2002).

4. See note 3.

5. Thomas J. Watson Jr., *Business and Its Belief: Ideas That Helped Build IBM* (New York: McGraw-Hill, 1963).

6. From Wikipedia, the free encyclopedia, Thomas J. Watson.

7. Terrence E. Deal and Allan A. Kennedy, *Corporate Cultures: The Rites and Rituals of Corporate Life* (Reading, MA: Addison-Wesley, 1982).

Chapter 2: Has-Beens, Wannabes, and Heroes

1. This is a variation on a quote that has been attributed to everyone from Werner Erhard to Gloria Steinem to the always quotable Anonymous. Larry gets the credit here because he is my friend.

2. Troy Woverton, "Pets.com Latest High-Profile Dot-Com Disaster," CNET News.com (November 7, 2000).

179

3. Bob Murphy, a motivational humorist from Nacogdoches, Texas, called this the Noah Principle.

4. Chuck Martin, "On the Mind: Technology Spending," www.darwinmag.com (April 2003).

5. Timothy L. Keiningham, Terry G. Vavra, Lerzan Aksoy, and Henri Wallard, *Loyalty Myths: Hyped Strategies That Will Put You Out of Business—and Proven Tactics That Really Work* (Hoboken, NJ: Wiley, 2005).

6. Max DePree, *Leadership Is an Art* (New York: Doubleday Currency, 1989).

7. Larry Bossidy and Ram Charan, *Confronting Reality: Doing What Matters to Get Things Right* (New York: Crown Business, 2004).

8. Bethany McLean and Peter Elkind, *The Smartest Guys in the Room* (New York: Portfolio, 2004).

9. Sam Walton with John Huey, *Made in America* (New York: Bantam Books, 1993), p. 80.

10. See note 9.

11. Larry Bossidy and Ram Charan, *Execution: The Discipline of Getting Things Done* (New York: Crown Business, 2002).

12. Janet Lowe, *Jack Welch Speaks* (New York: Wiley, 1998).

Chapter 3: Pursue the Best over the Easiest

1. Roger Von Oech, *A Whack on the Side of the Head: How to Unlock Your Mind for Innovation* (New York: Warner Books, 1983).

2. Carl Sewell and Paul B. Brown, *Customers for Life* (New York: Doubleday Currency, 1990).

3. Matt Haig, *Brand Failures* (London: Kogan Page, 2003).

Chapter 4: Leverage the Power of Partnerships

1. Remarks from Lincoln's "A House Divided" speech, June 16, 1858, on acceptance of the nomination for U.S. Senator for the State of Illinois.

2. Tom Rath and Donald O. Clifton, PhD, *How Full Is Your Bucket?* (New York: Gallup Press, 2004).

3. Timothy L. Keiningham, Terry G. Vavra, Lerzan Aksoy, and Henri Wallard, *Loyalty Myths: Hyped Strategies That Will Put You out of Business—and Proven Tactics That Really Work* (Hoboken, NJ: Wiley, 2005).

4. Maureen Minehan, "Restoring Employee—and Investor—Confidence," Strategy @ Work, Watson Wyatt Worldwide (September 2002).

5. Dilbert was created by Scott Adams. For more information, contact United Media 212-293-8500 or reprints@unitedmedia.com.

6. Trust Factors @ Work™ study conducted by Pennington Performance Group and Pilat—NAI. Copyright 2004 by Pennington Performance Group. All rights reserved.

7. You can download the executive overview on the Trust Factors @ Work™ Study at www.resultsrule.com.

Chapter 5: Focus the Energy

1. Coach John Wooden with Steve Jamison, *Wooden: A Lifetime of Observations and Reflections On and Off the Court* (New York: Contemporary Books, 1997).

2. Sirota Survey Intelligence surveyed 3.5 million workers at 237 large U.S. and foreign-based companies in 2005. See www.sirota.com for details.

3. Corey Rosen, John Case, and Martin Stabus, *Equity: Why Employee Ownership Is Good for Business* (Boston: Harvard Business School Press, 2005).

4. See note 3.

Chapter 6: Show the Courage of Accountability

1. Michael Jordan, edited by Mark Vancil, *Driven from Within* (New York: Atria Books, 2005).

2. Ram Charan, "Why CEO's Fail," *Fortune* (June 21, 1999), www.fortune.com/articles/0,5114,374594,00.html.

3. Mark Murphy, "Why CEO's Get Fired," *Leadership Excellence* (September, 2005), p. 14.

4. "Poor Performance in Government: A Quest for the True Story," U.S. Office of Personnel Management, Office of Merit Systems Oversight and Effectiveness (January 1999).

5. Marcia Dunn, "NASA Vows to Purge Bad Managers," *Associated Press* (April 13, 2004).

Chapter 7: A Love Affair with Results

1. "Agar-in the Future," *Fast Company*, FC Now: The Fast Company Weblog (September 19, 2003).

2. Jimmy Cox, "Nobody Knows You When You're Down and Out," song written in 1925.

3. Dan Ackman, "Excellence Sought—And Found," Forbes.com (October 4, 2002), www.forbes.com/2002/10/04/1004excellent_print.html.

4. Merrill R. Chapman, *In Search of Stupidity: Over 20 Years of High-Tech Marketing Disasters* (Berkley, CA: Apress, 2003).

5. Carol J. Loomis, "The Sinking of Bethlehem Steel," *Fortune* (April 5, 2004), pp. 176–187.

6. Thomas J. Watson Jr., *Business and Its Beliefs: Ideas That Helped Build IBM* (New York: McGraw-Hill, 1963).

7. Jerry Useem, "Another Boss, Another Revolution," *Fortune* (April 5, 2004), pp. 112–124.

8. Michael V. Copeland, "Stuck in the Spin Cycle," *Business 2.0* (May 2005), pp. 74–75.

9. Andrew S. Grove, *Only the Paranoid Survive* (New York: Currency Doubleday, 1996).

10. Arie P. de Geus, "Planning as Learning," *Harvard Business Review* (March/April 1988).

11. Jena McGregor, "Competing on Culture," *Fast Company*, no. 92 (March 2005), www.fastcompany.com/magazine/92/clear-leader-extra.html.

12. David Moore, "Duncan Has What It Takes, and Then Some," DallasNews.com (June 24, 2005).

13. Marc Gunther, "The MVP of Late Night," *Fortune* (February 23, 2004), pp. 102–109.

14. Mark Cuban (Blog Maverick), "The Sport of Business" (March 12, 2005).

15. Karen Schwartz, "Tangy Touch in the Sky," *Associated Press* (November 17, 1996).

Index

Index

Index

Index

Wheeler, Cass, 170
Whitehead, Ron:
   culture, 55, 56, 57, 95, 110
   innovation, 162
   story telling, 119
Whole Foods, 2

X

Xerox, 154, 158, 159, 160,
   161

Z

Zulke, Brad, 95, 109, 170

About the Author

Randy Pennington is a resource to leaders who expect results. He consults with and presents to organizations that want to create a culture committed to results, relationships, and accountability. For information regarding presentations, seminars, leadership retreats, and consulting service, please contact:

Pennington Performance Group
4004 Winter Park Lane
Addison, Texas 75001
(972) 980-9857 or (800) 779-5295 (U.S.)
www.penningtongroup.com
www.resultsrule.com